WOODY HERMAN AND STUART TROUP

THE
WOODCHOPPER's
BALL

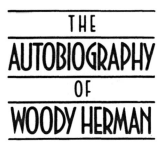

THE
AUTOBIOGRAPHY
OF
WOODY HERMAN

LIMELIGHT EDITIONS
New York

First Limelight Edition April 1994

Photographs curtesy of Ingrid Herman Reese.

Library of Congress Cataloging-in-Publication Data

Herman, Woody, 1913-1987.
    The woodchopper's ball : the autobiography of
Woody Herman / Woody Herman and
Stuart Troup. — 1st Limelight ed.
        p. cm.
    Originally published: New York : E.P. Dutton, 1990.
    Includes discography.
    Includes Index.
    ISBN 0-87910-176-8
    1. Herman, Woody, 1913-1987. 2. Jazz musicians—United States--Biography. I. Troup, Stuart. II. Title.
ML419.H45A3 1994
781.65'092—dc20
[B]   94-2586
                                                                         CIP
                                                                         MN

To Jack Siefert

ACKNOWLEDGMENTS

Woody's health began to fail midway through this project. Its completion was enabled with the help of many of those who loved him; in particular, the following: Jack and Mary Siefert, Chubby Jackson, Nat Pierce, Ralph Burns, Don Lamond, Polly Podewell, Ingrid Herman Reese, Gene Lees, Erwin Sherman, George Simon, Billy Bauer, Red Rodney, Milt Jackson, Red Mitchell, Major Holley, Bill Byrne, Frank Tiberi, Alan Broadbent, Harold Danko, John Fedchock, Lynn Seaton, Richard Stolzman, Tony Outhwaite, and Peter Levinson.

CONTENTS

Contents

Sixteen pages of photographs follow page 100.

PROLOGUE

The deputy from the Los Angeles sheriff's office drove up the steep, winding beauty of Hollywood Boulevard on Thursday morning, September 3, 1987. He stopped at the front door of Woody Herman's low-slung, deceptively simple-looking home.

He carried an eviction notice.

Woody was oblivious to the scene. He was in bed, his familiar surroundings crowded with the requirements of his condition: oxygen tanks, a wheelchair, and a full-time nurse. A tube was delivering the nutrition his seventy-four-year-old body no longer had the ability to swallow.

The deputy rang the doorbell.

Woody couldn't hear it. He was fading in and out of

consciousness, as he had since coming home a week earlier from his fifth hospital stay in seven months. The resiliency with which he survived a half-century of musical trailblazing had been overtaken by the punishing residuals of the journey, congestive heart disease and emphysema.

His daughter, Ingrid, took the envelope and read the court order. It required that the premises be vacated in five days.

Woody lay one floor below in his sanctuary, on the center level of the spacious four-bedroom home tucked against the mountainside. He and his late wife, Charlotte, had purchased the house in 1946 from Humphrey Bogart and Lauren Bacall, for cash, when the Herman band was riding its highest crest. He lost Charlotte to cancer in 1982, and he lost ownership of the house to the Internal Revenue Service in 1985. The government had seized the property and sold it at auction to mitigate the huge tax bill the IRS claimed Woody owed from the mid-1960s. He and Ingrid were permitted to remain as tenants, at $1,150 a month.

But he was no longer able to pay. The little cash he had left after the IRS began taking its weekly cut in the late 1960s had been wiped out in the past seven months by the cost of medical attention, nursing care, and medicine. Woody was four months behind in the rent.

Ingrid telephoned her lawyers, Kirk Pasich in Los Angeles and Leonard Garment in Washington, D.C. With the three-day Labor Day weekend approaching, there wasn't much time to act. The attorneys conferred and Pasich went to Superior Court the next morning, Friday, to request a temporary restraining order. Judge Ricardo A. Torres decided that the property owner, William Little, required more than a few hours of notice, and he set a hearing for Tuesday.

With their legal path stymied until after the holiday, the lawyers decided to publicize Woody's plight. By nightfall that Friday, much of the world was stunned by the news that

Woody Herman—whose dedication, droll wit, and sense of musical adventure had enabled his orchestras to survive the collapse of the big band era, the crush of rock and roll, and a twenty-year income tax battle—was impoverished, on a life-support system, and about to be unmercifully uprooted from his home.

The response was compassionate, financial, and swift. Saul Levine, the owner of radio station KKGO-FM, said he would pay the $4,600 in back rent. Help was tendered by the celebrated, among them Frank Sinatra, Peggy Lee, Tony Bennett, Rosemary Clooney, and Clint Eastwood. And spirited support, which would later be manifested in contributions and the receipts from musical tributes, was offered by the many whose love Woody had engendered during more than fifty years of relentless, swingful excursions through every city and tank town in the country.

Reporters and cameramen milled about the house throughout the weekend, searching for an update and hoping for a glimpse of Woody. But the centerpiece of the drama remained unaware. Because of her father's pride and the tenuous state of his health, Ingrid ordered those in the house to protect him from any word of the predicament.

But Woody found out somehow on Monday.

"He told his nurse he wanted to get up and come out to the living room," Ingrid said.

The cameras gave the world its first glimpse of his frail condition. Instead of traumatizing him, the news, coupled with the corresponding outpouring of love and assistance, led to a noticeable improvement in his condition and spirit.

"It made him feel good knowing that people cared," Ingrid said.

The following day, Tuesday, Ingrid and attorney Pasich went to Superior Court. Judge Torres worked out an agreement with landlord Little that, with the past-due rent paid, allowed

Woody and his daughter to remain in the house until 1989.

"I'm happy," Little was reported to say after the hearing. "I don't like problems. I'm glad they can get some help. It shouldn't be a problem in the future."

For Woody, the future was only seven weeks long.

1
EARLY DAYS

I was listening to some kind of music constantly, from the beginning. My father, Otto, was a terrible ham. He saw in me the possible fulfillment of his love for show business, and he worked with me, teaching me songs, from the time I first remember seeing him. It wasn't long after I learned to walk that he was also coaching me to dance.

He would have loved working on the stage, instead of as a shoemaker at the Nunn-Bush factory in Milwaukee. He had a great collection of recordings at home, and he sang along with them. He even bought a player piano and supplied it with all the available piano rolls.

Otto was of German descent, but born in the United States. My mother, Martha, came to Milwaukee from Poland when she was an infant. I was their only child. They were kind and beautiful. They let me try to do anything I wanted, and if it didn't work out, they were sympathetic.

During my eighth summer, Otto decided I was ready to launch the career he never had. He brought me to an audition for a kiddie revue, and I got a part with a low-budget operation that included six or seven other kids and a mature woman, an old actress who played a schoolmarm with us.

I was on the road.

The kiddie revue was part of a package that was booked into theaters with a silent movie based on a Booth Tarkington story. Our group staged a skit, with music and dancing, before the film. My high point was my comedy efforts.

We traveled around Milwaukee, moving into upper Wisconsin and Michigan, but always staying within a couple of hundred miles of our home base. The operation was booked by Ed Weisfeldt, who was the manager of a Milwaukee movie house. Weisfeldt was a talented, savvy guy who coached us. We had a good conductor who accompanied us with a fiddle, and sometimes he added local musicians.

I took a few piano lessons, meanwhile, but I wasn't much interested in that instrument. I tried the violin, too, but I didn't like it any better.

"You'd better learn to play something," my father warned me, "or I'll break your neck."

I decided to try a saxophone and, with the earnings from that first summer on the road, I bought an E-flat alto sax, silver with a gold belt.

"You're going to have to play clarinet, too," my music teacher told me. "It's much more difficult, but you'd better get one so we can start working on it." I did, but the sax was the important instrument at that time, and the one that occupied most of my concentration.

My father, meanwhile, continued to broaden my song

repertoire, even adding some risqué material. In fact, one of those tunes—"Oh Gee, Say Gee, You Ought to See My Gee Gee From the Fiji Islands"—came in handy much later. Late in the forties, we were having some problems with Capitol Records because of meager sales. During a discussion of the problem one day, I said, "Look, I'll make you a couple of sides and I won't even bring in the band." They were curious.

"Get a record date in the next couple of days," I said, "and I'll take care of the rest."

I went to the Hangover Bar and Grill, which was on Sunset Boulevard, and I picked up a few guys who weren't too loaded to speak. I took them to the studio, and we did "Oh Gee, Say Gee." Capitol shipped more records that week than they had in a long time. But by the second week, the networks banned the record because of what they considered to be risqué lyrics. The line that damned it was "She wears a lot of leaves to protect her from the air." The flip side, I think, was "Rose of the Rio Grande." I picked my own name for the recording— Chuck Thomas. Those are my two middle names, Charles Thomas, Woodrow Charles Thomas.

Along with the coaching from my father, and the music lessons, I began to study dance at a school run by Roselie Edwards, who was a friend of my parents. She once conned me into playing the part of a dancing rooster at a children's ballet recital, dressing me in a feathered costume that drove me crazy. I was more interested in tap dancing, however, and I moved to other teachers.

I loved sports, and I tried to participate in everything. But I wasn't very good at things like baseball. So while my best friend, Ray Sherman, and other buddies were at the ball field or the gym, I was usually practicing music. Ray and I were the same age and very close, like our families. Ray's mother, whom I always called Aunt Julia, assisted at my birth. Ray's brothers, Erwin and Dan, remained lifelong friends.

My folks changed houses in Milwaukee often, sometimes more than once a year. One of the more interesting places we rented was an old summer home on Humboldt Avenue, in a suburban area that was about as far north as you could go in Milwaukee. The property, owned by the Schlitz brewery family, extended about three-fourths of a mile, to the shore of the Milwaukee River. The winter there was terrible, and we had stoves in every room. But the summer was fantastic, because I slept in the tower of the building. You had to go about four flights up a big winding staircase, and then there was a special riser that took you into the tower. That seemed pretty romantic. We shared the house with another family, and I shared the tower with the other family's oldest son, who was much older than me. We could see all the huge trees throughout the property from the tower. Below the trees were zillions of wild violet plants, and at the river's edge, there was a little boat landing from which I would jump in.

My parents weren't quite as thrilled with our various housing accommodations. My mother decided we could do better if she went to work. After my father got her a job with him in the shoe factory, we got better housing. I gained some anxiety, however, being alone at home in the afternoons.

The worry disappeared with the arrival of summer, when I went off with another kiddie revue. But the tours led to a new problem. When I returned to class in the fall, the teachers and school administrators figured that my parents were nuts to let me work in show business. And I was having a difficult time getting permission from juvenile court to have working papers. I was performing only while school was out. But the school officials were nonetheless annoyed with the idea and were delaying the court's approval of my papers. Their negativity bugged me even after the working papers came through, and I decided to do something about it.

I was only ten, and in the fifth grade, but I managed on

my own to transfer to St. John's Cathedral School in downtown Milwaukee, where I had heard the administration and teachers were more interested in individuals.

By that time, my musicianship, coupled with my singing and dancing, had made me a bookable act. The kiddie-revue days were over. I was able to play theaters as a single on a year-round basis, performing locally on school nights and sometimes traveling to other towns on weekends, often with my mother along. Eventually, I even played in some vaudeville houses in Chicago, billed as "The Boy Wonder."

With me on the same bill was a comic and a four-woman chorus line, singing bawdy songs. We often played two theaters a night, two shows at each theater, week in and week out.

Being a show business act gave me some kind of glow. I tried not to be too self-impressed, but it was a gas to walk by a theater and see my name in lights, and to collect as much as fifty dollars a week—a powerful income in the early twenties. My parents held the salary for me in a bank account, and saw that I had spending money.

As my ability increased, I became more interested in musical form than in show business flavor. I began collecting a few records, one of which featured an eight-piece group called The Washingtonians, led by Duke Ellington. It was the first time I ever heard what sounded to me like jungle music, and it knocked me out. I was impressed by the originality of the sounds and the different rhythm patterns.

It was tough to find recordings then of what I considered jazz. There were some Red Nichols records that I could handle very nicely, because he had some great soloists.

I began to take saxophone and clarinet lessons from a jazz-oriented teacher who wrote out choruses for me. He had his own little band that played at one of the local hotels, and I took at least one lesson a week from him.

Jazz was becoming more of an influence also through one of my high school buddies, a piano player named Al Mack. Al's older brothers, both of them priests, were also pianists. The oldest, who later became a monsignor, was a classical player, and the middle brother was Tony, who wore straight clothes to play jazz on gigs around Milwaukee. Tony was a beautiful man who taught me some harmony and theory. He also taught Al Mack to play in the Earl Hines style. It was through Tony that I became aware of Louis Armstrong, who had cut some sides with Hines. Hearing Armstrong made you a believer in what was swing.

Tony Mack later went to Rome to serve on the Vatican staff. And if anybody had encouraged him, I'm sure he would have played a little jazz right there.

In 1925, at age twelve, I decided I wanted a career playing jazz. So I announced to my parents that I was retiring from show business and, in the vernacular of the day, I was going to be a hot player.

They almost went into a dead faint.

When they recovered, the reaction on their faces was, "How is he going to make a living that way?" For them, the connotation of playing jazz was to perform with bums. Being in the theater was fine. But being a jazz musician wasn't exactly the future they had hoped for for me. Nevertheless, they said, "Go ahead, you can try it."

In my freshman year at St. John's Cathedral High School, I got my first steady job with a band of mature guys at a gig somewhere out in the county. One of the guys picked me up and we played until four in the morning on most days of the week. The hours didn't interfere with my getting to school at eight in the morning. But the sister teaching my class wasn't happy about my nodding off during class, and she showed her annoyance by sending me to the principal's office often.

My sense of what jazz was about increased considerably

when I found recordings by the Mound City Blue Blowers. That group was led by William (Red) McKenzie, who sang and blew through tissue paper and pocket comb in trumpet-imitation style. The featured players included Coleman Hawkins, Jack Teagarden, Eddie Condon, Gene Krupa, Muggsy Spanier, Jimmy Dorsey, Pee Wee Russell, and Glenn Miller, who also arranged some of their pieces. Hawkins' tenor sax solos, in particular, were a revelation.

I studied those solos by Hawkins, listening to them over and over. Erwin Sherman would come over to the house and crank up the Victrola while I tried to emulate the licks played by Hawkins or Frankie Trumbauer.

My jazz education was enlarging, but things weren't going well at school. Then, late in my second semester, the nun who was my science teacher also became my mentor.

Sister Fabian Reilly was an angel who believed that a musician, even one who played jazz, was a very good thing to be. I was always a little behind in my work because of my musical activities. When I was sent to the principal's office, she always arrived first to cop a plea for me. Whatever my problem, she could help me work it out.

"Just stick to your music," she said. "It's the best thing for you. You'll learn the other things."

Erwin Sherman recalls:

Woody was playing the road houses that ringed the Milwaukee area. One was called the Blue Heaven, on Green Bay Avenue, which is in the heart of the northside now, but it was outside of Milwaukee then. He also played Pick's Club Madrid, and a place on Muskego Lake, about 20 miles or so out of Milwaukee. And the Modernistic, which was in the fairgrounds on the west side of Milwaukee. He'd go as far away as Oshkosh and Waupacka, but they were mainly weekend gigs because he was still going to school.

When he was about sixteen, his car broke down west of Madison, about 150 miles from Milwaukee, on the way back from a gig with a group led by Joey Lichter. He called me, because he couldn't get his folks, who were out for the evening. I kept calling his house all evening, and I finally got Uncle Otto. We went out there together—me driving and he sleeping all the way. We got there at three in the morning, and we had to tow Woody's car—it was a Whippet—all the way back to Milwaukee. After the car was repaired in a couple of weeks, he was on the road again with Lichter.

Sister Fabian supported and saved me all through my high school days. In fact, we corresponded for years after I left Milwaukee and we would get together when I would pass through. I performed for her students and once, after giving me a frantic call concerning a building crisis at the school, I brought in the band to play a benefit at the auditorium. From then on, I tried to perform there at least once a year.

Sister Fabian would have seen me through to graduation, as well, if a bandleader named Tom Gerun hadn't come along in 1931, during my last semester in high school.

2
ON THE ROAD

Tom Gerun's band was playing at the Schroeder Hotel in Milwaukee when he called me, just a couple of months before my eighteenth birthday. A few of his musicians had heard me in Joey Lichter's band, and had recommended me. I went over to the hotel, and Gerun and I talked about what I could do and what he needed, which basically was a tenor player. The deal was made.

The band left town right away for Chicago, and I followed a few days later, chugging at twenty-five miles an hour to break in the new engine in my Whippet. We played the Chez Paris there and then moved to the William Penn Hotel in Pittsburgh for a few weeks.

It wasn't long before we were headed for San Francisco, where Gerun was best known. When we got there, we played the Noon Club. Then we moved into a place called the Bal Taberin for a long stay.

We were mainly a good entertainment orchestra, rather than a jazz band. Almost all twelve members would sing at one point or another. We had some of the better players in town in the saxophone section, which eventually included Al Morris, who later became a movie and recording star as Tony Martin. I played tenor mostly, and I doubled on baritone sax and clarinet.

Coleman Hawkins, whom I had never met, had made my tenor playing impressive. Few people in San Francisco had heard of Hawkins, no less realized that I was emulating his revolutionary solos from those records with the Mound City Blue Blowers.

As a singer, I was influenced by Russ Columbo and Red McKenzie and, later, Lee Wiley. I was inspired, too, by some who weren't thought of as singers, such as songwriter Harold Arlen, who sang on dates with Red Nichols, and Jack Teagarden.

One evening at the Bal Taberin, the cast of a new musical called *Nine O'Clock Revue* came in for an opening night party. And I spotted a beautiful dancer with flaming red hair. Her name was Charlotte Neste, and we were attracted to each other from the start.

The romance continued by phone and letter after she returned to Los Angeles. When I went to visit her there about a year later, Tom Gerun asked me to try to find a new girl singer for the band. I knew a couple of music publishers there, and they helped me arrange for an audition session. More than fifty singers showed up and I listened to them all before deciding on Virginia Simms.

She joined Gerun's band and she worked out fine. But later, when we were about to go east on tour, she decided to stay in San Francisco. Tom hated to lose her, but he recommended her to the bandleader coming into the Bal Taberin—

Kay Kyser. He hired her, changed her name to Ginny Simms, and she became one of the leading pop singers of the thirties and forties.

Charlotte, meanwhile, was rehearsing in a second musical that was headed for San Francisco, with Barbara Stanwyck playing the lead. It wasn't much of a show, unfortunately, and—after it played San Francisco—it had a disastrous tour across the country. By time the show reached New York, it was in utter collapse.

Our romance, however, was going strong, despite being limited to phone conversations. But I wasn't about to consider marriage until I became a bandleader, which I had already begun thinking about.

A year or so later, the Tom Gerun band hit Chicago again for a stay at the Granada Cafe, on the South Side. It was also known as Al Quadbach's, because he was the front man for the club, which was rumored to belong to Al Capone. We followed Paul Whiteman's Orchestra in there, and we had to play for the various entertainers who were also on the bill, which included comic Fuzzy Knight.

After work one night, Fuzzy and I and Steve Bowers, the bass player with the band, went out to hear the Earl Hines Orchestra, which was playing at the Grand Terrace, a large after-hours place. Picking up on the sounds of the great bands on the South Side was the thing to do then, and we arrived at about four or five in the morning, still dressed in our band tuxedos. I was even wearing my homburg. I liked being dressed properly. I was described once in San Francisco as "the kid, drunk and dressy, and always a gentleman."

We were in a semi-hilarious mood and Fuzzy was waving his hand, a finger of which was decorated with a big diamond ring. That combination, plus the roll of more than a thousand dollars that Fuzzy flashed, didn't go unnoticed.

The trouble began while we were driving back to our hotel

in my Pontiac roadster, with Fuzzy next to me and Steve in the back. We stopped for a red light and a big black sedan pulled up next to us. Three guys jumped out and started opening our doors and banging on the car. They couldn't seem to do much with us because we were well oiled and weren't responding too well. We scuffled with them from our seats and one guy decided the noise we were making might attract attention, so he slugged me on top of the head with his fist. But the homburg saved me. The hood got frustrated, pulled a pistol, and fired a bullet toward the floorboard of the car to scare us. My right leg unfortunately was in the way, and the bullet went straight through my calf and dropped on the floor.

I got out of the car, dragging my leg behind me, and moved off to find help. I located a policeman a couple of blocks away, told him I had just been shot in the leg and that the hoods might still be back at the car with my buddies. The cop took a whiff of my breath and said, "Boy, you've been drinking. You better go home."

When I got back to the car, I found Fuzzy and Steve waiting for me. The hoods had left without getting anything. We took my car back to our hotel and called a doctor. He put me into one of those South Side hospitals that took care of things like a small shooting. And I got out the next day.

Gerun was a likeable man who treated us well. One night in Pittsburgh, he received a telegram on the bandstand that said he had been wiped out in the stock market. He stuffed the wire into his pocket and we continued playing. When we finished the last song of the evening, he threw a big party for the band. That took some kind of courage.

After about three years with the band, most of it in San Francisco, I began to get antsy to start a group of my own. In mid-1934, I left Gerun and went to Milwaukee. I knew a few agents, and I talked to people at MCA, but they weren't encouraging. The only thing left to do was hunt for another job.

I found two, one right after the other. The first was with Harry Sosnick, who had an important band that did a lot of radio work. We did broadcasts from theaters and hotels in the Midwest and Far West. Our itinerary included the Chase in St. Louis and the Cosmopolitan Hotel in Denver.

On the advice of MCA, I left Sosnick after a couple of months to join the Gus Arnheim band. It was good advice, indeed, because Arnheim's subsequent cross-country tour of theaters brought me to Pittsburgh. The Isham Jones Orchestra happened to be playing there at the same time.

3
WITH
ISHAM JONES

I got a telephone call at my hotel one day from a member of the Isham Jones band, who said I should speak to his boss.

Isham Jones was big league, and his band was more musical than Arnheim's. Jones had earned a national reputation through his compositions. I was nervous at our meeting, but Isham made it easy.

"Is it true that you can sing and dance and play good saxophone?" he asked.

"That's what I try to do," I replied.

"Well," he said, pausing for a moment, "you'd better join us."

He made arrangements for me to join the band in Denver a few weeks later. But when I got there, he had forgotten about it. The tenor player I was to replace hadn't been given notice.

I was worried plenty at first, because Isham had a reputation of being tight with the dollar, and paying salaries to two guys when only one was working was a distasteful idea to him. But he gave the tenor player an extra two weeks' pay to go home with.

My salary with Isham was in the neighborhood of $125 a week, about the same that I got with Arnheim. From that, we had to pay all of our road expenses, including travel, but the hotels were dirt cheap then. I was able to get a first-class room in 1934 for something like a buck and a half.

I did a little of everything except dancing with Isham's band—singing, playing saxophones and clarinet. He had a quite successful and identifiable tenor soloist named Saxie Mansfield, so I played baritone sax most of the time. His main singer was Eddie Stone, who was well known to Jones fans. When I was called upon to sing, I did things such as "Basin Street" and some ballads that I also recorded with the band.

Isham was a fantastic song writer. Among the hits he wrote were "I'll See You in My Dreams," "It Had to Be You," "The One I Love Belongs to Somebody Else," "There Is No Greater Love," "Swinging Down the Lane," "You've Got Me Crying Again," "When Your Dreamboat Comes In," and "On the Alamo." He cared about his charts. If you made an error in your part—missing a cue slightly, for example—he was forgiving. But you couldn't miss any notes. If you did, it would be you and him out in the back.

He loved his players, but he wouldn't interfere in any of the little problems that arise among band members on the road. If a couple of the guys got into a hassle and started fighting, he would stand by and watch them.

My romance with Charlotte was still relegated to letters and phone calls. I couldn't see marriage yet, especially after watching the difficulty married players had in the Isham Jones band, where wives were barred from traveling or from attending a lot of things. Those were the rules of the day, and only a leader could change them.

Not long after I joined the band, Isham started talking about his new ranch in Denver, where he wanted to raise turkeys. His songs had made him wealthy, and the band seemed to be only a second thought to him. He wanted to get off the road and live a new life.

Five of us, realizing that the band might be close to a breakup, began discussing the idea of forming a cooperative. Besides me, there was Saxie Mansfield, arranger and flugelhorn player Joe Bishop, bassist Walt Yoder, and Nick Hupfer, a violinist I had known in Milwaukee who had changed his name to Harper. Nick was also a pretty good arranger.

A small group including Yoder, Mansfield, and myself had already recorded for Decca, under the name of the Isham Jones Juniors. So the people at Decca were aware of me and were especially impressed with my singing. In March 1936, we had cut eight sides, five of them with vocals by Virginia Verrell or me, with a group that also included Chelsea Quealey on trumpet, Sonny Lee on trombone, Howard Smith on piano, George Wartner on guitar, and Walter Lagesone on drums.

When Isham's moment of decision occurred in the summer of 1936, while the band was in Texas, we were ready. We had a contract with Decca—a rare thing in those days—and it gave us a sense of solidity. We also took James Noble into the cooperative. Noble, whose nickname was Jiggs, was an arranger on Isham's staff, and he later prepared charts for our record dates while we were busy playing gigs. Jiggs turned out some pretty good arrangements, including "The Golden Wedding," which did well for us four years later.

The other members of the Isham Jones band picked up various jobs. Two or three of them went with Ray Noble, who was then a big hit at the Rainbow Room in New York. Gordon Jenkins got an assignment to write for a show that was opening on Broadway, and he took two or three players with him.

Our group had decided to start in New York, where we could pick up other players and begin auditioning the band for bookings. We had discussed for months exactly what we wanted to do.

We agreed to call ourselves The Band That Plays the Blues. The reason was obvious: Playing the blues was the best thing we knew how to do musically.

The guys agreed that I would be the leader, even though I was the youngest. They figured that I could handle it best because of my early show-biz background. And they knew I would be a more personable front man than Isham. He was a good musician and a great songwriter, but in front of the band he was something I had no intention of being: a flop.

4

ON OUR OWN

Being a leader was all the excuse I needed to send for Charlotte. She came to New York, where we were married by a justice of the peace on September 27, 1936. We spent our honeymoon in the city, visiting various clubs on 52nd Street—the Onyx, the Famous Door, Leon & Eddie's, Jack White's.

The band, meanwhile, needed to add seven players to our core of five. It wasn't easy to find them, with nothing to offer a player besides stock in an orchestra without a gig. But if a guy was nutty enough, he would join us. When we needed to make a decision about somebody, we held a meeting, sometimes all of us going to the men's room, where we could talk in private.

The band started rehearsing in a hall that the management of the Capitol Hotel let us use without charge. A few weeks later, The Band That Plays the Blues got its first booking, in Brooklyn Roseland, at Fulton and Flatbush Avenues—sort of a tryout for the Roseland Ballroom in Manhattan.

We opened on Election Night, 1936, with only a dozen or so arrangements in the book, so we made up tunes—so-called head arrangements—on the job. One of those head arrangements, a riff based on the blues, evolved into "Woodchopper's Ball." Everybody contributed something to it, but we didn't name it until later. And we cut our first two recordings for Decca: "Wintertime Dreams" and "Someone to Care for Me."

I was singing, playing some alto sax and mostly clarinet, which was a hot instrument during that period.

The pay scale at Roseland was $50 a week for the guys, $75 for me as leader. Big deal: leader. It was a job I couldn't afford. When somebody from the press came in, I had to pick up his drink tab. And a nut from the *Brooklyn Eagle* showed up one night and wanted to dance with the hostesses, at so much a dance. After a few of those incidents, I started making deals with the manager of the place, explaining that I couldn't pay my rent.

The main thing was that we were a hit. After three weeks there, Lou Brecker, who owned both ballrooms, moved us into the Roseland Ballroom in Manhattan. The blues were the best thing we knew how to play, but we had to do a lot of fighting to play them. The management preferred that we play mostly dance music—fox trots, rhumbas, and waltzes—to satisfy the dancers.

We stayed at Roseland for seven months, and for a while the Count Basie Orchestra was booked to play alternately with us from a second bandstand. But Basie didn't remain there very long. What may have curtailed his stay, as a matter of fact, were the dance hostesses. They would have meetings and report to the management about which bands played good music for dancing. They reported that they could dance to us, but they were having difficulty dancing to the Basie band. We were playing with a heavy two-and-four beat, and Basie was playing swing in four. The dancers of that period needed a heavy metronome; they couldn't feel the real swing of Basie.

George Simon, who chronicled the big band era, recalls:

I first heard the band in December of 1936, after they moved into Roseland *in Manhattan. My review in* Metronome *appeared the following month. What was very interesting was that the Basie band was on the opposite stand. And I gave the Herman band a higher rating than the Basie band, for which John Hammond never forgave me. But Bill Basie, and Buck Clayton especially, said that I was absolutely right. The Basie band played out of tune.*

I gave Woody an A– and Basie a B.

Charlotte and I, meanwhile, began married life in an apartment on Bleecker Street in Greenwich Village. Shortly after we moved in, someone gave us a wire-haired terrier, and walking that pup several times a day from a fifth-floor walkup kept us in pretty good shape. Charlotte was heartbroken when the pup died of distemper that first year, and I began shopping for another one right away. From that point on, we usually had a cocker spaniel.

We moved from there to a ground-floor apartment in Jackson Heights. By our standards then, the place was huge, with two bedrooms and a big, open area in back, which opened onto a nine-hole golf course. We were close to LaGuardia Airport, which we would visit for a meal in the main dining room when I had a day off. The guy who operated the restaurant later ran a chain of hotels around the country, including the New Yorker in Manhattan, and we eventually worked for him there.

We signed a management contract with General Artists Corporation during the Roseland engagement, but it didn't exactly signal a big break. When the gig ended, GAC told us bluntly they couldn't do much for the band. I spent a lot of time sitting in the GAC outer office, often with Glenn Miller, trying to see somebody.

I was twenty-four years old and optimistic. Glenn was a little older and sour. He had already blown a ton of money with three bands, and he was full of sad stories. GAC apparently didn't think very much of either of us at that point.

Roseland had given our band a taste of honey, but it would be a long time before things got that good again.

One of the engagements we got the following summer, however, turned up something a lot more important than an opportunity to work. It initiated my introduction to Jack Siefert, a man whose warm friendship and support would help sustain me all my life.

Jack Siefert recalls:

I was living in the Philadelphia area, and a woman from Milwaukee named Pauline Traub—Aunt Pauline, we called her—became a neighbor. I used to play my one record too loud, and one day she said to me, "You like music, don't you, Jack." And I said, "Yeah." She said, "My nephew's a musician, his name is Woody Herman."

At the time, Woody was playing with the Harry Sosnick band, which was broadcasting on a show out of Chicago every Wednesday night. So I began listening to it. I felt that I practically knew Woody because of my neighbor.

The kids in my neighborhood would do anything to get down to the Jersey shore during the summer. Money was scarce and cars were few, but somehow or other we all managed to get to the shore over the big weekends. Later on, we would run record hops during the winter, playing our own records to raise money for a place at the shore during the summer.

The first weekend that I arrived in Wildwood, New Jersey, was the Fourth of July, 1937. Woody's band was booked into Hunt's Ocean Pier on the boardwalk.

I went to see him, and said, "Mr. Herman, I'm Jack Seifert, I'm a friend of your Aunt Pauline."

"Oh, Aunt Pauline," he said. "Stick around, kid. We'll have a milk shake together."

At intermission, that's what we did.

He was five years older than me. I was just out of high school and I thought he was like God. He was booked there for about two weeks, I think, and we often went down to the beach to sit and talk. Sometimes we had softball games, with his band versus us.

Guy Hunt was a very good businessman; he owned all the theaters and amusements in Wildwood and was very generous to local charities. On Sunday afternoons, he arranged for the band to set up directly on the beach, on plywood sheets, and do radio broadcasts. That would stimulate interest and the kids, instead of going back to Philly early on Sunday afternoon, would stick around and go to Hunt's Pier and dance to the music of Woody, then drive home at night. We told people that we stayed late to beat the traffic, but the real reason was to hear the band. Woody was very popular and developed a very loyal group of fans from the Philadelphia area, a great many of whom vacationed at the Jersey shore.

Guy Hunt and Woody became very good friends, and when the engagement was about over, Guy said to him, "Where are you playing after this?"

Woody said, "No place."

"You want to play here for one more week."

And Woody said, "I'd love to."

Guy hired a plane to go up and down the beach hauling a sign that said: "Held over by popular demand: Woody Herman."

I was down there that summer for maybe four weeks with him. After that, I took my vacations and traveled with the band, wherever he was, at the Meadowbrook in New Jersey or any place in the east.

In the forties, when the band had some difficulties traveling because of gasoline rationing, I was with him at the Adams Theater in

Newark, New Jersey. Guy Hunt's Ocean Pier burned down in Wild-wood, and I showed Woody the newspaper clipping.

"Gee," he said, "I'll have to send Guy a telegram."

It said: "Dear Guy. Sorry to hear about your fire. But where the hell did you get the gasoline?"

5
THE SCHRIBMANS

Without financing, we were not going to get very far. It was suggested that we contact Charles and Si Schribman in Boston. Their operation was to finance bands at engagements in their own ballrooms or in hotels, which didn't pay an up-and-coming band what it needed to survive. But the Schribmans would arrange for air time on network radio during those appearances, and the air shots in turn provided the exposure that created bookings. When a band had enough bookings for a tour, it would move out of the New England area, take care of itself financially, and repay the Schribmans. Those hotel engagements were consequently the lifeblood of the big bands.

If it cost, for example, a thousand dollars a week to underwrite our stay at a hotel in Boston, that became the Schribmans' investment. They didn't do much of the on-the-road bookings, except for some fill-ins around New England while we were gathering enough engagements to make a road trip worthwhile. We'd be living in Boston meanwhile, and driving somewhere in the New England area every day. When we finally had enough advance bookings for a tour, we headed out of Boston to different parts of the country, playing anything we could get.

George Simon recalls:

I first heard about the Schribmans when I was living in college in Boston, leading a band called George Simon and His Confederates. That was about 1932. They were booking bands then.

I knew them both, but I knew Si better than Charlie, because he was always on the scene. Charlie Schribman was the quieter of the two, a kindly sort of guy. Si was sort of a big gruff guy. He would just barge ahead and do what he thought was right. He apparently had a tremendous instinct to do the right thing. The guys told me that he would go around at night to the various places in the Boston area and collect money for bookings. His pockets would be bulging with cash. Then he'd take what he got in one place and use it to pay a band in another place. It was unbelievable.

But he was completely honest. I never heard a bandleader ever say a word against him. He and his brother supported many of the big bands, and they saved Artie Shaw and Glenn Miller. Those air shots were terribly important.

But The Band That Played the Blues had difficulty living up to its name, especially in the South and the Southwest. At one place in Texas, the manager sent a note to me that said, "You will kindly stop playing and singing those nigger blues."

That's the way it was.

The pay on our bookings was usually based on a percentage of the house, with a minimum guarantee. With enough radio broadcasts preceding our tours, we could gross a lot of money. Radio was stronger for us than anything we've had since, even television.

Those getting support from the Schribmans included Artie Shaw, Red Norvo, and Glenn Miller. For a while, several bands were living at the Avery Hotel in Copley Square in Boston at the same time. The hotel manager was a terrific guy who would let our bills ride for weeks. He helped us a great deal, giving us gasoline money when we had to ride to a job. He was probably glad to lose us for a few days.

One night while partying in the hotel, Glenn joined us. He had made a pact with his wife that he was through drinking. He couldn't drink and he knew it; it would turn him crazy. But on this particular night, Glenn not only joined us, he brought along some liquor to supplement the little already in our possession.

It became a real roaring party. We even locked one of my guys out on the fire escape in his underpants, and it was snowing like hell. We were doing numbers like that. By three or four in the morning, everybody had just passed out or gone to bed.

The desk clerk rang Glenn a couple of hours later to remind him that he had to go three hundred miles in the snowstorm to play a one-nighter. Glenn was fuming, partly from the hangover but mostly at me. In his mind, I was responsible for his drinking and staying up most of the night. He got dressed and started beating on everybody's door. Then his guys went outside and found their cars wouldn't start.

My first realization of all this activity was when Glenn started beating on my door. I grunted a reply, and he came into the room with a bellhop, who was carrying a big tray of chipped ice and a bottle of booze.

Glenn slapped me awake. Then he handed me the bottle of booze and said, "Either you drink the booze or I give you the ice!"

I just lay there, hungover and helpless.

"Give me the ice, man," I mumbled.

He tossed it over me and the two of them stomped out. I was lying in a deep freeze, but after the night we had it felt good.

A couple of days later, Glenn called and insisted I take his lead trumpet player.

"You need this guy," Glenn said. "You need a little more power in your band."

"I do?"

"Yeah," he said, "you need him."

It didn't take long to find out why Glenn had sent him. The guy had to have a drink before he could say hello.

We had become the house unit for Decca, having to record any tune that was a hit on another label. Mary Martin sang with us for a while in late 1938, and she and the Andrews Sisters recorded with us that December and the following January in New York.

Walt Yoder, meanwhile, came up with the title for the "Woodchopper's Ball." It happened one day after he had gone to see the Sportsmen's Show at the Boston Garden. While wandering around there, he came upon a group of wood-choppers competing against the clock for prizes. That's all there was to it. And our most famous head arrangement got its name.

We recorded "Woodchopper's Ball" for the first time on April 12, 1939, and it was really a sleeper. But Decca kept re-releasing it, and over a period of three or four years it became a hit. Eventually it sold more than five million copies—the biggest hit I ever had.

The flip side of "Woodchopper's Ball" featured Mary Ann McCall on her first outing with us, singing "Big-Wig in the Wigwam." Mary Ann stayed only through the end of that year, but she returned late in 1945 on the recommendation of song-plugger Juggy Gale. During that second stint, she made many recordings with the band, including "I Got It Bad and That Ain't Good," "Detour Ahead," "Romance in the Dark," and "Wrap Your Troubles in Dreams." That last one showed that she was truly a great jazz singer.

The band was playing major rooms, such as the Meadow-brook in Cedar Grove, New Jersey. But nothing up to that time compared with the thrill of performing on Manhattan's 52nd Street at the Famous Door. There was no real bread, but the exposure and publicity were worth a fortune.

6
BROADWAY

The band's reputation was growing faster than we realized. For example, after recording "Blues in the Night" in Los Angeles on September 10, 1941, we were busy touring in the Midwest and had no idea of how the record was doing. When we returned to New York City to open at the Strand Theater, everything seemed normal until the middle of the first show. I called "Blues in the Night," and the moment I sang the first line—"My momma done told me"—the joint fell down.

We had cut that record for Decca soon after the *Blues in the Night* movie was released. Jimmy Lunceford's band played the song in the movie, with a big concert arrangement. But it didn't get much air play. We did it more simply. The writers of the song, Harold Arlen and Johnny Mercer, were there and

Johnny got into the act. In the little call-and-response thing in the middle of the song, he sang those "my momma done told me" answers. You can barely tell the difference between when I stop and he starts, because we both sounded like barroom singers.

The funny thing was, we spent more time on the flip side of that record, which was "This Time the Dream's on Me." We worked for hours on it, and had the whole band singing and making backgrounds. That side, of course, was heard maybe twice and "Blues in the Night" turned into a smash.

The reception at the Strand was cheery news, and a far cry from the way we were received on Broadway later at the Paramount Theater. We opened there with a stage show that included Bob Hope. He was making his first New York appearance since becoming a hit in Chicago, where he had set attendance records at the Chicago Theater. Hope had an act that also featured his wife and Jerry Colonna, and he was used to breaking it up.

But business was rotten because we were booked with a so-so movie. The Paramount management went crazy trying to turn things around. Between shows, they had us making personal appearances around town, trying to get our pictures into the papers. But nothing helped.

For years afterward, Hope would hiss the title of that picture. He would say: "It was called *The Magnificent Fraud*. No wonder we died."

We stayed at the Paramount five or six weeks that first time, all the while fearful that we had blown any chance of being booked there again. To add to our anxiety, Hope was on edge because his act was being punctuated by a noise that sounded like a razzberry. The noise began to occur intermittently on the third or fourth day, during one of the morning shows. A few times the razz even competed with his punchlines.

The management had security guards and cops, even schoolchildren, trying to find the culprit. Hope was certain it was sabotage, and he was going wild. Arguments broke out offstage and there was a generally nervous atmosphere. After he had suffered much humiliation, a leakage in the sound system was discovered just in back of the big screen behind us on the stage.

When the band got another chance at the Paramount later, we rewarded the management with good business. We played there often after that, sometimes accompanying a Bob and Bing *Road* picture, and wound up staying for periods of from ten to twelve weeks.

The manager of the Paramount, Bob Whiteman, made some important contributions to the well-being of my family life. Charlotte loved the theater, and when we were in New York, she would go to a different show during every free moment. She knew that getting a single ticket was easy. Whiteman changed the band's schedule at the Paramount so that I could go with Charlotte to catch opening night of *Oklahoma!*

But a new problem was developing. We were doing five, six, and sometimes seven shows a day, seven days a week, beginning shortly after nine in the morning and finishing after midnight. I was concentrating so hard on making a success of the band that I hadn't paid much attention to such logical things as food. I was suffering from malnutrition and nervousness.

My lawyer set up a couple of meetings with a psychiatrist, a European guy. He helped me a great deal. In the process, however, we transferred the anxiety to the management of the Paramount and other theaters that we played subsequently.

The psychiatrist suggested that my anxiety was being caused, in part, by my arrival an hour or so before show time.

"Stop hanging around the theater," he said. "Instead, just walk in at the last minute and jump in."

It worked. But the Paramount management almost had heart failure the first few times I stepped into the theater and onto the stage, just as it was rising out of the orchestra pit.

The news of how well we were doing on Broadway led to more theater bookings around the country. But between those theater engagements, we were still scuffling for locations, such as hotels in which we might get some radio time. Radio was everything—the single most important link to bookings and good crowds. The broadcasts sustained the bands by keeping them before the public. Without radio, we might do well in Cleveland and the following week die in Columbus.

We were headed in all directions, using cars and a converted milk van. The trips would knock us out. After the war began, however, gasoline rationing forced us to use trains, and we would get some rest between engagements. Nevertheless, we would often close in one city one night and have to open the next morning in another town. Early shows were the norm everywhere, because our music was the entertainment of youth. Kids would skip school to hear us before the prices changed after noon.

We still called ourselves The Band That Plays the Blues, but in the newspaper advertisements and on the recordings we had become the Woody Herman Band. Among the changes was the addition of a female trumpet player named Billie Rogers, a good performer from Montana who also sang very well. She stayed from 1941 to 1943, when she left to start her own band.

Beginning in 1942, we began losing guys to the Army, including some of those who co-owned the band with me. My lawyer advised me to pick up their stock.

When it came time for me to take my physical for the draft in New York City, the band was playing in Detroit. GAC, which was booking us, was concerned about losing me. One of its representatives suggested that I stop off at an Army training camp in Maryland for a pre-physical on my way to New York. I took a train to Washington, made my way to the camp, and looked up the young doctor I was told to see.

"Have you ever had anything wrong with you?" he asked.

I said, "No, not really, but I recently had a hernia operation."

He touched the wound, and said, "Boy, they did a good job on that one." Then he started me on all sorts of tests, which took the entire day to complete. I was getting fed up with it, going from one doctor to another.

Every once in a while, the first young doctor would stop by and say, "I hope we can find something, because I don't believe you should be in the Army."

"Why not?" I asked.

"I'm here doing work," he said, "but you're doing more good on the outside than you could ever do in the service."

I certainly wanted to believe him, so it wasn't difficult to.

He was upset. He said, "I'm going to shake that hernia again. Get up on that chair."

While I was standing on the chair, he lunged at me with his finger and I went right up to the ceiling.

"Well," he said, "now you've got a hernia on the other side."

When I recovered, he issued me instructions before I left for the physical in New York.

"When you get to New York," he said, "don't take a cab. Walk from Penn Station to Grand Central. And when you get there, jump up and down a little bit, to be sure it's down and hanging."

Sure enough, the doctors took one look at the hernia, and I was rejected.

The band hadn't yet become a huge financial success by early 1942, but we had carved a number of significant notches with such hits as "Woodchopper's Ball" and "Blues in the Night," a few movie shorts that helped establish our identity, and what became a major recording with Bing Crosby, "Deep in the Heart of Texas." We used the so-called Woodchoppers, a septet taken from the full band, to back Bing.

The financial insecurity didn't have much of an effect on my marriage. Charlotte and I were both experienced with the show biz roller coaster, and we anticipated the lows even while hoping for highs. When we were poor, we managed to button up. But when we had even moderate prosperity, we lived to the hilt.

One way to have Charlotte share in any success was to surprise her with something expensive. After buying her a fur stole, I decided that every successful man's wife should have a natural ranch mink coat. She was flabbergasted. So were the lawyers who managed my business affairs, Goldfarb, Mirenburg and Vallon. Their reaction was: "Has she got something on him?"

Charlotte became pregnant and she left our Queens apartment temporarily to stay with her parents in Los Angeles. Our daughter, Ingrid, was born on September 3, 1941.

While Ingrid was still very small, we arranged to have a big reunion with our parents at a Christmas party in our Jackson Heights apartment. We had all the trimmings, including a couple of bonuses. One of them arrived from Milwaukee with my parents. When I was a kid, my father had built a mechanism to keep the Christmas tree turning—it had a little motor with the revolutions geared down—and he brought along all the works and set it up with the lights and a music box.

The second surprise was for Charlotte. I had noticed a certain look on her face one day when she eyed a Russian white fur in a store window. On Christmas Eve, I bought it. When she opened the box that evening, you could hear her for miles. My lawyers really flipped out.

7
INSIDE MOVES

With the personnel changes caused by the draft, we began to play differently, and I was looking for different kinds of arrangements. Most of our charts had been done by Jiggs Noble, Joe Bishop, Nick Harper, and Gordon Jenkins. They were fine writers, but I felt that we were in a rut; we weren't progressing.

Among those I turned to were Dave Matthews, who turned out such outstanding charts as "Four or Five Times," "Do Nothin' Till You Hear From Me," "Perdido," and "Cherry." And Dizzy Gillespie wrote three or four pieces for us, including "Down Under" and "Swing Shift."

Dizzy said I was the first guy to pay him $100 for an arrangement. I remember the first time I sent him over to my lawyers' office to pick up a check. My lawyers were good business people, but they were square. Dizzy went up there in full regalia—goatee and bebop glasses and so forth. And he was cleaning his nails with a stiletto.

I got a call from Goldfarb: "What the hell have you sent us now?" He said he didn't know whether to call the cops.

"Just give Dizzy a check for a hundred dollars," I told him.

Dizzy also subbed with the band for a week when we played the Apollo. I took the liberty of advising him to concentrate on arranging and writing tunes, which was where I thought his talent really lay.

"Forget the horn, stick to writing," I said. Thank God he ignored me.

During that period of the band's transition, I moved the family to the West Coast, into an apartment at the Garden of Allah, a fancy housing complex on Sunset Boulevard, with a bar, a dining room, and a pack of resident actors.

Charlotte was wonderful and mercurial, with a mad sense of humor that was sometimes sparked by jealousy. One of her chances to display it occurred when we spent three days with friends at their Malibu beach house. The woman was an excellent chef and Ingrid played with their son at the beach every day. It was a great visit and, as we were saying our goodbyes, I kissed our hostess very gently and thanked her. That's all there was to it.

We got in the old Cadillac and started back toward Los Angeles just as a blinding fog came in. I could barely see the road, so I stopped the car at the side and jumped out to wipe the windshield. While I was out there, I could hear the engine revving up, and I moved out of the way. Charlotte had slid into the driver's seat and she suddenly drove off in a blaze.

There I was, thirty miles from nowhere. I walked to a lamppost nearby, sat down at the base of it, and lit a cigarette.

About two minutes later, a cab stopped right at the base of the lamppost. The driver stuck his head out the window and said, "Can I help you, sir?"

I jumped in and told him, "Here's a double sawbuck, and I got some more if you get me to the Garden of Allah as quick as you can."

The guy was a born race driver. The fog didn't bother him and we drove into the Garden of Allah parking area just as Charlotte was pulling the car into the other driveway. I ran into the bar and ordered a drink. The martini was in front of me when Charlotte walked in, and when she saw me she shrieked in disbelief.

It was that mad sense of humor that helped keep us together. I was very proud of her, but she could also put me in some trying positions, not all of which had laughable endings.

After playing one evening at the Sherman Hotel in Chicago, we made our usual stop at an all-night place on West Street, on the near North Side. It was about two in the morning, and the place was crowded. We went to the bar for a drink before ordering food and greeted the patrons we knew.

All of sudden a woman in back of me put her hands over my eyes, let out a shriek, and said, "Hello, Woodsy!"

Without a word, Charlotte started picking up everything she could get her hands on—glasses, ashtrays—and began tossing them at the pink-mirrored bar. Before long, she had wiped out most of the booze and made a shambles of the mirror.

I sat quietly at the bar with my drink. I wasn't about to be lured into the fray. Everyone tried to appease her, but she just kept hurling things. Finally, this heavyset man, whom we knew casually, told her, "Charlotte, you're such a lovely gal; why are you doing this?"

She turned and gave him a shot in the belly, and he fell right to his knees.

• • •

By late 1942, the draft was causing personnel changes every day or every week. A year later, such players as tenor saxophonist Vido Musso, trombonist Eddie Bert, pianist Jimmy Rowles, and trumpeter Billy May had come and gone.

Then two guys named Chubby helped turn everything around.

8
A THREE-RING CIRCUS

The law firm of Herman Gold-farb, Mary Mirenburg, and Mike Vallon were handling the band's business affairs in the early forties. Goldfarb, whose nickname was Chubby, had worked as credit manager for the Conn Company, which made musical instruments. He knew thousands of musicians.

Goldfarb was aware that I was looking for a bass player in 1943, and he kept leaving messages for me to "Call Chubby."

I called Chubby Goldfarb and said, "What's up?"

"Call Chubby," he said.

"What do you mean, 'Call Chubby.' I thought you were Chubby. Who the hell *is* Chubby?"

"Chubby Jackson," he said, "a very good bass player with

Charlie Barnet. He's a great performer and he would be good for you."

Chubby Jackson recalls:

A guy calls me one day and says, "This is Chubby. How would you like to join the Woody Herman Band?"

Chubby? I figured it was a joke, so I hung up on him.

Then one day Woody calls and says, "This is Woody Herman. Did you get a call from my lawyer, Chubby Goldfarb?"

Chubby Goldfarb was right about Chubby Jackson, of course. He was not only a terrific bassist and the band's cheerleader, he was also a great help in filling our ranks with other fine musicians. He would get out to hear everybody and come back yelling about one player or another.

Chubby first helped us get singer Francis Wayne. The two of them recommended pianist Ralph Burns, who joined us in January 1944, from the Charlie Barnet band.

Ralph Burns was an especially important acquisition—a fine piano player and a great writer. He gave me the liberty to change his charts if he thought I could improve them. But I hardly ever touched them. As late as 1986, when I was planning the Fiftieth Anniversary Concert at the Hollywood Bowl, Ralph sent me a tape of a new piece called "The Godmother," which he dedicated to Charlotte. He said once again, "If there's anything you want different, do it." He always trusted me.

Ralph Burns recalls:

I joined about a month after Chubby, but I stopped playing piano regularly with the band after a couple of years. By that time, Woody had signed with Columbia and gotten the Wildroot radio show, so I said, "Why don't I just write and follow the band around?" I would meet the band every week before the Tuesday night show and turn in my charts.

I worked exclusively for Woody for about five years, and continued to write for the band for another ten while writing for singers and other bands at the same time.

I think my first chart for Woody was "Happiness Is Just a Thing Called Joe." I had done that one for Charlie Barnet, when Mary Ann McCall was singing for Charlie. With Woody, I wrote it for Francis Wayne to sing. I have no idea how many pieces I did altogether, but it was at least two or three a week during the first few years. I wrote "Bijou" in 1945, the same year I did "Summer Sequence" while spending the summer at Chubby Jackson's house in Freeport, on Long Island.

Woody taught me so much about writing. His big thing was that it wouldn't swing if there were too many notes. A lot of stuff is overwritten when you're young and eager. Sometimes he would edit the arrangements during rehearsals or on the bandstand.

He took "Bijou" as is. But when I got a little complicated on a chart, he always tried to simplify it. Sometimes I didn't feel good about the changes, but he knew what he was doing, and that's the way you learn. It was never offensive; he would maybe take out the brass here, or something like that, so that it would swing.

The band was very headstrong, but Woody kept us under control. He was a master at pulling everything together. We were like a big pro football team, crazy and wild and one big wonderful bunch. He would let us get a little crazy because he knew the music would come out. But when things got out of hand, he'd say, "Cool it."

He always knew his limitations as a musician. It was never "I'm the king." It was more like "I'm the father." He was a master psychologist. He knew how to manipulate people, and he manipulated us into giving our all.

It was a fantasy world for us, because people thought differently about bands then, probably the way they think about rock groups now. It took me years to recover from it. If you were a jazz musician playing with Woody Herman, you were almost like a movie star. You'd get into a town and people would be lined up outside waiting for your autograph. It was a wonderful trip.

Trumpeter Neal Hefti also followed Ralph from the Charlie Barnet band. Among the great pieces he wrote for us were

"Half Past Jumping Time" and "The Good Earth." He contributed brass figures to many of our head arrangements. That was very important in such pieces as "Caldonia," where the unison trumpet part was a high point. Neal and Francis Wayne fell in love, married, and left to join Harry James in 1946.

Flip Phillips, who had subbed in the band for Vido Musso in 1943, was skeptical about joining us. He was playing tenor sax with Russ Morgan's band. Morgan had been involved with jazz musicians in New York, but he had moved to a very commercial sound. Flip felt that Morgan's was a more stable operation. Even after he first joined us, he returned to Morgan two or three times. But he joined us for good in mid-1944.

Budd Johnson, the great saxophonist who had been Earl Hines' musical director for many years, also wrote for us and subbed a few times in my band. Budd was Mister Experience as a writer and a player with a big Coleman Hawkins tone. I didn't always feel that all my men were as competent as they should have been, and Budd was the kind of guest who could help tighten things up. It was one of my wiser moves.

At about the same time, a few members of Duke Ellington's band were unhappy about not getting enough attention. I felt the complaint was unjustified. I knew how Duke operated and, if there had been reason for anybody in his band to get more attention, he would have made it possible. He was that kind of guy. They were unhappy nonetheless, and three of them—tenor saxophonist Ben Webster, trombonist Juan Tizol, trumpeter Ray Nance, and alto saxophonist Johnny Hodges—approached me about recording with us.

It didn't bother Duke. He told me: "If you can make a buck, go ahead." I jumped at the opportunity.

Ben Webster first recorded two tunes with us, on November 8, 1943: "The Music Stopped" and "Do Nothing Till You Hear From Me." We went into a studio again nine days later and cut "Who Dat Up Dere, Who Dat Down Dere," which

Duke Ellington had something to do with the writing of. We were looking for material with broad appeal. Decca was giving us more and more liberties since we proved we could sell a few records.

"Who Dat Up Dere" was an overnight success. Ben didn't get billing on the record, but those who were into music recognized his distinctive sound. Duke took some heat from the NAACP about that tune, and he called and asked me what I could do to get it off the air. I told him, "I can't do anything about it on radio. All I can do is not play it on the bandstand."

It was the second time that one of my recordings had caused a fuss. The first was in 1939, when we cut "Blues on Parade," which was written by Toby Tyler. It apparently was a takeoff on Rossini's "Stabat Mater," which had been used in the Catholic Church on Good Friday. I had no idea about that, but I began to get threatening letters from the church about playing the piece. The church wanted me to get the recording off the market, which I couldn't do. But a young friend of mine who was attending a seminary got me out of the jam. He was a big music buff and he learned, to my relief, that Rossini's music had already been banned by the church, which had decided it was too dramatic. Saved by the bell, but I sweated.

Tizol, Nance, and Johnny Hodges joined us for a World Transcriptions recording session on April 5, 1944 (later released on Coral, Decca, and Ajaz), when we cut "Perdido," which Tizol had written, and "As Long as I Live," "I Didn't Know About You," and "Blue Lullabye."

With our music more diversified in mood and sound, we were able to play the black theaters. In fact, we were one of only two white bands doing that regularly—the other was Charlie Barnet's—in Baltimore, Washington, and New York at the Apollo.

When our drummer, Cliff Leeman, decided to leave, I

decided to bring in Davey Tough, who was working in Charlie Spivak's band. Chubby flipped out when I told him. He and some of the other guys in the band remembered him as the drummer with Tommy Dorsey a few years earlier, and they felt Davey wasn't a modern-enough player. Also, they were all in their twenties, and Tough was older.

"I don't think that's what we need," Chubby told me. "We need a little sweetie who's gonna help the band."

"This guy Tough is very special," I said, but Chubby was unconvinced.

The day after Davey joined the band, Chubby came to me raving.

Chubby Jackson recalls:

I had made the biggest mistake in the world, because I became acquainted with one of the better generals of rhythm thinking. Dave Tough was totally brilliant. He tuned the drums to certain notes; he didn't believe in metronomical time; he thought we should move. Flip was right down the middle, so we stayed with him. Sonny Berman used to play behind the beat, so we'd cool under him. And Bill Harris played on top of the beat, so we'd go with him. But when it was ensemble it was Davey and myself. He insisted that I stand right next to him so I could watch his foot pedal and the movement of his hands. I learned an awful lot from Dave.

We were no longer The Band That Plays the Blues. Thanks to George Simon, the writer who chronicled the Swing Era, we were becoming known as Woody Herman's Herd. George had given us that name in *Metronome* a few years earlier, but it was just beginning to catch on.

George Simon recalls:

During the summer of 1944, as a G.I., I drove out to Pleasure Beach in Bridgeport, Connecticut, to hear Woody Herman's band. Caesar Petrillo [head of the American Federation of Musicians] had put through one of his seemingly regular recording bans. This had been a long one, so that most of us hadn't had a chance to keep up with the sounds of the bands. And even though I'd always followed Woody closely since late 1936, when I'd become a fan of his band through a friend of his, I had no idea that he'd put together the sort of group I was to hear that night. It was completely different from anything of his I'd heard before. I went absolutely out of my mind.

There was a wonderful alto saxophone player by the name of Bill Shine, and of course there were Flip Phillips, Ray Wetzel, Pete Candoli, Conte Candoli, Neal Hefti, and Dick Munson. The guy I thought was really unheralded in that band was Ralph Pfeffner. His playing was gorgeous. Because Harris was all that exciting, Pfeffner was another exceptional trombone soloist who never got the breaks he deserved.

My review in Metronome *came out in September of 1944. It began:*

> *"Before you can have a really great band," Woody Herman once told me, "you've got to be able to play really fine music all night long. You can't just coast along on a few good arrangements and then just play average stuff for the rest of the evening." Today Woody Herman's band qualifies in terms of Woody Herman's own exacting requirements, with no reservations whatsoever. . . . It can and does do everything. It jumps like mad, with either a soloist in the lead or the entire group attacking riffs en masse. And it can play really pretty, moodful ballads . . .*

Finally, after raving about the Davey Tough–led rhythm section, and about Flip Phillips, Bill Harris, Ralph Burns and others, the review concluded:

> *Yes, this is truly a great all-around band, this Woody Herman Herd . . .*

I called it the Herd because I was a frustrated sports writer, and I used to do alliterations: The Herman Herd, The Goodman Gang,

The Dorsey Dervishes . . . brilliant things like that. The Herd was the only thing that really stuck.

We were getting exposure in movies, although there weren't any I want to brag about. We made a number of short films, one in 1938 for Vitaphone and a few for Universal.

What's Cookin'? was our first feature film, in 1942—a routine comedy that also featured the Andrews Sisters. Two years later, we made two pictures: *Earl Carroll Vanities* and *Sensations of 1945*, with Eleanor Powell. And we played in *New Orleans*, which featured Louis Armstrong and Billie Holiday.

I had to do a little acting in some of the films, but not much. They were all nothing pictures, especially the stock Westerns we appeared in for Republic. Making the movies was hard work and the finished products were disappointing. But they helped make the band more identifiable.

Of the eight or nine feature-length films we were in, the only good-budget picture was *Wintertime* for 20th Century Fox, starring Sonja Henie, in 1943. We had an option to do a couple more for that studio, but an unfortunate incident occurred.

We had been on the picture for weeks. We recorded the music first and then sat around for a call so we could go through the motions for the camera. The guys, meanwhile, were out playing ball or doing anything to pass the time. In the evenings, we were performing at the Hollywood Palladium.

The studio suddenly decided it needed us twenty-four hours straight through for a couple of days. By the second day of that, I was worn out, and the guys were trying to amuse themselves any way they could just to stay awake.

They decided to get one of the alto players in the band loaded, a nice quiet guy named Chuck DiMaggio. In the middle of a take at four in the morning, DiMaggio heaved right into his saxophone.

That ended our options at 20th Century Fox.

By the middle of 1944, the band was a solid swing machine, beefed up in every department. Marjorie Hyams became our vibraphonist, and the rhythm section was ironclad with Chubby Jackson on bass, Ralph Burns on piano, Davey Tough on drums, and Billy Bauer on guitar.

Chubby Jackson recalls:

When I joined Woody in 1943, it was still The Band That Plays the Blues—an adequate dance band but nothing terribly impressive.

Little by little, he started leaning more toward a jazz concept. Woody was absolutely the man who gave me the full range of all my little eccentricities. And we had a devotion to him that could easily be called love. He was a great coordinator of musicians, because of his personality. He understood not to tell a new guy how to play. "Let him play," he'd say, "and adjust it." [Trumpeter] Sonny Berman, for instance, liked to play three choruses in a row. But we discovered that Sonny was best at the little shouts, the eight-bar fill, or a little chorus.

The band looked like everything we did was an ad lib. That was our reputation—"Oh, look at that, right on the spur of the moment." But each move was well planned. I was the buffoon, the first one to wear the beard, the different uniforms. I got the blame for it as years went by. I was the eccentric—"He's out of it." Nobody really knew that Woody had suggested, "Let's do this, let's do that." The numbers we did together, when he called me out front, turned into bizarre vaudeville.

For example, one of the numbers he had me doing was to put the bass across my knees while sitting down. Woody and I had a dialogue before we went into the music. My bit was always screaming, "WOODY HERMAN," and "YOWWW." I knew when to yell. Woody always said that I won the down beat *poll one year for yelling. I knew just when to yell, and the band would respond. We were all geared up to beat the Chicago Bears every night.*

We used to be in utter amazement of [trombonist] Bill Harris.

We'd wait for his chorus to come and wonder, "What is he gonna play tonight?" Every night was another challenge for him.

Ralph Burns was a genius of an arranger and a composer, very deep. Neal Hefti had a lighter flavor, but he could bounce your nose off. So we had the thrill of a very heavy symphonic classical guy who would write gorgeous things and another who would bounce you into the next state.

On one-nighters, Woody would often leave in the middle of the last set, and we would make up head arrangements. "Apple Honey," "Wild Root," "Northwest Passage," those were made up by the rhythm section playing four to eight bars to get into it. Then Flip Phillips would start to play, endlessly. Meanwhile, Neal would add figures. Then Bill Harris, and finally the ensemble.

The next night I would say to Woody, "We got one for you."

"Let's hear it," he'd say.

Little by little we were adding our own flavor. Woody never stopped us. He would be the coordinator. Sometimes it would piss us off that we had something great and he would cut the shit out of it. But we would make the record, and suddenly it was absolutely right.

He knew how to posture everybody in a very short time. He knew exactly when somebody should be playing. We started to realize that we were able to show as much genius as the boss wished. We had seven or eight guys who were winning polls every year. It was a big boost for Woody, business-wise, because the band was getting more popular.

We had a spirit on that bandstand that no other band possessed. Basie's band was a lay-back band, good ensembles. Duke's band was based on a lot of marvelous potpourri, with marvelous writing. But none of these bands had, like, the fire engines starting to go.

I was in and out of the band because the moment that I saved any money I would leave to start my own band. And I would fail miserably. Then I'd call Woody and say, "It's me." He'd say, "When do you want to come back?"

I only saw Woody get really uptight once. It was years later, in the sixties, when he was coming into the Metropole in New York.

They had hired me to be the relief band. I played the first set, and then I saw Woody down at the other end of the bar. I put down my bass, and yelled "Hey Wood," and we hugged. The boss of the Metropole was an unbelievable man. The bartenders and everybody were afraid of him. Woody and I talked while he was putting a reed in his clarinet. And the boss comes over and says, "Hey, c'mon man, let's go to work, what are you doin' here?"

Nobody talked to Woody that way.

"Excuse me?" Woody said, glaring at him.

And the guy said, "Yeah, you're Woody Herman, aren't you? Well I own this joint, so let's get on the bandstand. Talk to this guy later."

So Woody said, "I'll tell you, sir, you talk to [business manager] Abe Turchen from now on if you want to say anything to me. If you say the same thing to me again in the same tone, two things are going to occur. I'm going to turn around and tell my band to go home, and, number two, I'm gonna take this clarinet and break it over your fucking head."

I looked at Woody and, in all the years that I'd known him, I said, "Hey, is that you?"

He said, "Chubby, every now and then a man has to stand up and be a man."

Another time that he threw a great line at me was after my divorce. I was in terrible shape in Detroit, and he was coming into town. We got together in his hotel room.

He said, "All right, come on, what's the matter?"

"I really don't want to talk about it, Wood."

He said, "Look, I'm an amateur psychologist after leading a band for so many years, and you're my boy. So tell me whatever you want to tell me. Get it off your chest."

"Woody, I don't wish to talk about it."

And he said, "Thanks."

"Thanks?"

He said, "Look, I got enough going on myself. I would do it for you because of my affection for you. But being you don't want to talk about it takes a big load off my mind."

We were beefing up the band in every section.

Flip Phillips was joined in the reed section by Sam Marowitz on lead alto and John LaPorta. Pete Candoli came over from the Tommy Dorsey band to play lead trumpet. And Pete's kid brother, Conte, took a seat in the trumpet section during the summer of 1944, while he was still a teenager. I told him he could come back when he finished high school. And he did.

With some coaxing, we convinced trombonist Bill Harris to leave Bob Chester's band. Bill had also served with Benny Goodman, Gene Krupa, and Ray McKinley. He was a powerhouse who pulled the whole section with him. By the end of 1944, Sonny Berman added energy to the trumpets, and Shorty Rogers joined him the following year.

The band was like a three-ring circus. Chubby Jackson was doing his own number, jumping in the air, mugging and carrying on like crazy. And the five trumpet players paraded on the top riser, swinging back and forth.

When Tommy Dorsey was asked about the band, he said, "I don't know how they play, but they sure as hell are great dancers."

Sonny Berman finished his solo one night and, while they were swinging up there with their horns, he jumped down to the next level. His portly figure went right through the floorboard, and he was in wood up to his navel.

Sonny was a happy young man, with fire and feeling in his horn. His potential was enormous, and he might have fulfilled it if his heroin habit hadn't cut him down at the age of twenty-one, after he left our band.

Everybody in the band was trying to top each other, and Pete Candoli came up with one of our most successful gimmicks, which he initiated on his own one day. While we were playing "Apple Honey," he sneaked off the bandstand and put on a red and blue Superman outfit, cape and all, that his wife had made for him. We were playing the last chorus when he jumped out on stage in time to play his walloping passages. It brought down the house, and it remained part of our act.

Bill Harris, too, was famous for his bits. He was a great practical joker, continually finding gimmicks to use on and off stage. He had a little gizmo that would make fart sounds. I remember him in an elevator full of people, driving them mad with it at the Sherman Hotel in Chicago. And he would use it to break up the band on stage.

Bill wanted me to get a fellow in Philadelphia to make him a set of shoe cleats that locked on to the stage. That way he could bend all the way back, forward and sideways without falling, while playing trombone. But the guy in Philly was about to go out of business and didn't want to mess with it.

Once at the Paramount in New York, Bill and Sonny Berman got a monkey and put it in a dressing room on the seventh floor. Any publishers who wanted to show us songs were told they had to talk first with the new secretary in Room 702. When their knocking went unanswered, they would open the door and there was this fucking monkey swinging from wall to wall, with monkey shit all over the place.

Billy Bauer recalls:

I got there in the spring of 1944. The only guy I knew in the band was Flip, and he probably recommended me. He and I had written tunes together and we had worked together.

Woody was playing at the Meadowbrook in New Jersey. He called me and said, "I wonder if you'd come over and sit in with the band."

"Gee, Woody," I said, "you picked the wrong night." It was my daughter's birthday and we had a party going on.

So he said, "Go up to see Abe Turchen and sign a contract."

I joined the band a few days later in Detroit. The band was shrieking, and Woody let me play bombs. Davey Tough liked me. When we played in crammed quarters, he said, "You sit right here." After we got through one night, he said to me, "You know something, I only thought a Christian could play like that."

Eastwood Gardens in Detroit was an open-air place, and we were playing there once when it started to drizzle. They didn't want to cancel, so they moved the whole band under a shed, and all the people were jammed in there on top of us. The band just wailed that night. When we stopped, nobody said anything. The hair was standing up on my arms. I said to Davey, "Look." And he pulled up his sleeve and said the same thing.

I asked for raises a number of times, and got them. But one time, Woody said, "Well, let me think about it." We hit this town and Charlotte came to meet us, something she would do every once in a while. Woody said to me, "Bring the guitar to my dressing room." I did, and Charlotte was there. Woody took out his clarinet and said, "All right, come on, let's play." He started and I followed. We played away for about ten minutes. Then he looked around at Charlotte and said, "Okay, what do you think?" She didn't say anything. She just shook her head yes. I got the raise.

We had an incident once with Skippy DeSair, the baritone saxophone player. He was the kind of guy who would sleep on the floor so he wouldn't have to pay for his room. He owned a couple of apartment houses in Albany. On the road he would stop at pawn shops and pick up Conn instruments. He'd pay something like fifty dollars for them and go to the post office and mail them to Conn, and they'd send him a check for seventy-five, or something like that. Anyway, Skippy came up with this idea for guys in the band to pool their money for him to invest for us. But we didn't go for it.

Then he came up with this idea to sell little plastic penny whistles, classic black with a white mouthpiece, with Woody's name imprinted on them. He talked to Woody about it, and Woody said, "It sounds good, but I don't bother with that stuff. Speak to the lawyers who manage the band."

Skippy did, and he came back and said he had to find out how much it would cost to get a mold for the whistle. It was thousands of dollars. The lawyers called Skippy to sign a contract.

Woody said to Skippy, "Get yourself a lawyer. I don't want anything to do with it." So Skippy told us one day, "Hey, I signed a contract. I get five percent."

We didn't hear much about it after that, but we noticed later that, as we were playing, there were vendors going around with these whistles. Then we saw them in Gimbels. Skippy figured he was going to make a lot of money, but the whistle company pointed out that he was entitled only to five percent of what he sold. Woody told him again, "I told you to get yourself a lawyer." Then Woody told us, "Listen, ideas are a dime a dozen. To get them working is what counts. If Skippy had gotten a lawyer before he signed a contract he might have been all right."

Most of the guys were warm toward each other. We'd get together every night in one room or another. It was a happy band. When Roosevelt died, we were at the Sherman Hotel in Chicago. We got on the bandstand and played the Star Spangled Banner. It was a chilling moment. Then we packed up.

When we played the Paramount in New York for five or six weeks, we'd hang out in the dressing rooms between shows. Sonny Berman, Neal Hefti, and Shorty Rogers. Once we did a "Jack and the Beanstalk" recording for fun on an acetate machine for my daughter, Pam. It was Red Norvo, Chubby, and Sonny, and I was Jack. We wrote a whole skit, with Buddy Lester—the comic who was Jerry Lester's brother— narrating. Sonny did a very good Jewish accent, so on the other side they did the same story in Yiddish. I still have it.

Abe Turchen, who was the road manager, was quite a character. After we played in a fight arena in Birmingham, Alabama, one time, Abe had a big bag over his shoulder when he came on the bus. He looked like Santa Claus. And in the bag was the money.

I left the band a few months before he broke it up near the end of 1946. Chuck Wayne took my place.

. . .

Our national popularity was nourished in 1945 by our film appearances and our weekly Old Gold radio broadcasts in August and September, when we replaced the Frankie Carle band. The biggest shot in the arm, however, was signing with Columbia Records.

It was still wartime, and companies could press only a limited number of records for an artist before moving on to another artist. So I made a deal.

"Don't worry about the guarantees," I told Columbia. "Just give me as much publicity as your top two artists." The top two Columbia artists then were Frank Sinatra and Dinah Shore. Every time Columbia put an ad in a trade paper, I got one. That drove the other bandleaders crazy—Les Brown, Harry James. They couldn't figure it out. Sinatra would be on one page, Dinah Shore on the other, and I would be on the next: "Columbia Records presents . . ." We became Number One in the country because of that as much as anything. It pushed us to the very peak of popularity.

"Laura" was the first side we recorded on our first Columbia date, and it was also our first release. I had seen the movie, heard the theme and liked it. Harry James was Columbia's big band then, and he thought he had it sewed up. He recorded it a few days after us, but Columbia scrapped his and released ours.

I had arranged with Johnny Mercer to sing his lyric. We were performing at the Meadowbrook in New Jersey when we went into the studio in New York on February 19, 1945, to make the cut. It became a smash hit. Columbia had a gold record made as a special gift to me, even though the record hadn't really sold a million copies. It couldn't, because the companies weren't allowed to press that many. But Columbia gave me the gold record as a token. Over a period of years, it finally did sell a million.

On that session, we also recorded "Apple Honey," which

was one of our many head arrangements on which everybody contributed—Pete Candoli, Bill Harris, Flip Phillips, Ralph Burns, and Neal Hefti. It was based on the chords of "I Got Rhythm."

We recorded "Caldonia" and "Happiness Is Just a Thing Called Joe" a week later. I had heard about "Caldonia" through music publishing friends and some guys who had seen Louis Jordan perform at the Paramount. I sent Ralph Burns there to listen.

"Yeah! We've got to do it," he said. It was twelve bars, up-tempo, with the shout at the very end—"Caldonia, Caldonia, what makes your big head so hard!" We made up everything else in that chart with a head arrangement. We were the only band doing that sort of thing at the time, and it gave us something different to say. The kids were picking up on it and that contributed plenty to our success.

"Happiness Is Just a Thing Called Joe" was the best thing that Francis Wayne ever sang with us. She showed an awful lot on that song, which she had been doing in a nightclub act before she joined us.

Our next session was March 1, and we recorded three more of what were to become some of our biggest numbers: "Goosey Gander," "Northwest Passage," and "I've Got the World on a String."

"Goosey Gander" was completely a head arrangement. We needed a fourth side on the record date, and that's what we came up with. The beginning is based on "Shortnin' Bread," but like so many other things, it goes into the blues. The screeching trumpet over the ensemble was Pete Candoli, and that little extra drum tag that Davey Tough put on the end was one of those things we liked to do in one way or another. We hated to cut arrangements short, the way most of the big bands were doing, so we usually let about three more things fall.

"Northwest Passage," too, was a head arrangement that

evolved on the job. It began with that little thing around rhythm and vibes and we kept adding and changing it around. The ensemble shout is Neal Hefti's.

I always liked "I've Got the World on a String." It was the first arrangement that Ralph Burns wrote at Chubby Jackson's request. I used it throughout my career.

Two more of our hits were recorded in August: "The Good Earth" and "Bijou." Neal Hefti wrote "The Good Earth," and we broke it in on the job. It's a wonderfully constructed piece that every young arranger could learn from. My clarinet tag was ad-libbed, another way of not cutting our endings too short. Ralph Burns wrote "Bijou" for Bill Harris, and it really established Bill as a major instrumentalist. I gave it the "Rhumba a la Jazz" subtitle because I was trying to explain why we were abusing the Latin rhythm. I guess you could call it a "stone-age bossa nova."

Virtually every time we went into the studio, we came out with at least one hit. On the September 5 recording date, we did "Your Father's Moustache." The melody was by Bill Harris and the ensemble chart belonged to Neal Hefti. Buddy Rich did a terrific job, subbing for Davey Tough, and Red Norvo played vibes.

Almost all of our records were selling to the maximum number of wartime pressings. A number of bands were doing as well, but we were causing more excitement with the Columbia promotion and the popularity of our presentation.

In October 1945, we became the first band in years to sign for a weekly network radio show. It was sponsored by Wildroot, the hair tonic and shampoo company, and the added exposure helped us set attendance records at ballrooms and theaters everywhere.

Neal Hefti, meanwhile, composed "Wild Root," which was based on "Flyin' Home," and we played it for months before we named it after our radio sponsor.

The domino effect was incredible. The Herd was voted the best swing band in the *down beat* poll, and it won awards from *Metronome* and *Esquire*. The 1945 *Esquire* New Star awards went to Flip Phillips for tenor sax, to Chubby Jackson for bass, to Bill Harris for trombone and, the following year, to trumpeter Pete Candoli and pianist Ralph Burns. Bill, Chubby, and Davey Tough also won polls conducted by *down beat* and *Metronome*.

But by the time Tough was selected, he had become too ill to work regularly. So we sent for Don Lamond.

Don Lamond recalls:

I was in Washington, D.C., which was my home at the time, when Sonny Berman recommended me to Woody at the end of 1945. My own small band had just finished a long gig and I was jobbing around. Woody's band was in Norfolk, Virginia, when I got the call from Abe Turchen, who was the road manager. He said, "Don't bring your drums, because you can use Davey's."

I went out to the airport and got on a plane, but we were just sitting and sitting there for a long time. There was a big flood down South, from Washington all the way to Georgia. The plane couldn't take off because it couldn't land in Norfolk.

After about forty-five minutes or an hour, we got off and I went down to Union Station to get on a train. But it took us hours to get to Norfolk because the flood prevented the train from running on the regular tracks. By the time I got to Norfolk, the band had left for Raleigh, North Carolina. By time I got to Raleigh, they had left for Charleston, South Carolina.

Back on the train. The railroad had put on extra runs with steam locomotives because of all the servicemen coming home, and with the windows open we were black with soot. The train pulled into Charleston at about seven or eight o'clock at night, early enough to make the gig. But the train yards were in chaos because of all the traffic. So the train sat in the yards until it got to be about ten.

I finally got off in the train yards and walked through to the station. But by the time I got to the gig, the band had left again. I stayed overnight at the YMCA, which, like the train tickets, was at my own expense. I hadn't received any advance.

I was about ready to give up. I figured, well, Woody's probably got another drummer by now. But I took a chance and followed them to Augusta, Georgia. When I got there, I asked around for the main hotel, and I telephoned, asking if they had a Sonny Berman registered.

"Yes, he's here," somebody answered.

God almighty, I finally found them.

When I spoke to Sonny, he said, "Where the hell have you been?"

I said, "I've been trying to catch this damn band for a week."

I got to the hotel and I was black from the soot. Abe Turchen said, "Why didn't you take a private plane from Raleigh?"

I said, "Now you tell me."

When I played that night, the first tune that Woody pulled up was called "Half Past Jumpin' Time." I knew the damn thing because Neal Hefti had written the same chart for the Sonny Dunham band. The guys must have thought, this guy can really read.

Woody's was an easy band to play with. I had quite a bit of experience with Boyd Raeburn and some other big bands, so a lot of the time I didn't even look at the music; I just felt my way through it.

That band was powerful, with Flip Phillips, Bill Harris, Conrad Gozzo, and Sonny Berman. I first knew Sonny when he was seventeen, in Louis Prima's band. Then he went with Sonny Dunham, then with Boyd Raeburn. I left Raeburn to return to Washington and Sonny, meantime, went to Harry James and then to Woody. He died in 1946 at the age of twenty-one.

I had a good relationship with Woody. He never would strain you up, like Benny Goodman would. He gave me a free hand. He was a good guy to work for.

When Woody broke up that band at the end of 1946, I was living in Santa Monica, because Jimmy Rowles had talked me into coming out there. Jimmy, who was the pianist with Woody when the Army drafted him in 1943, was given his old job back when he was discharged early in 1946. It was the law. He replaced Tony Aless, who came up to me and said, "Jeez, I got my notice."

I was in the Bradford Hotel in Boston when I saw this guy walking down the corridor with dark glasses, and I said, "Who's this character?" It turned out to be Jimmy. We played a ballroom that night and all I had to hear was about eight bars before he became a real favorite of mine. A magnificent player.

Things were terrific. But the best was yet to come.

9
AT THE TOP

A young man who worked for a music publisher in New York had some conversations in 1945 with my attorney, Howard Goldfarb, about Igor Stravinsky. The young man knew the composer and Goldfarb decided he would try to interest Stravinsky in writing something for our band.

I didn't think it could happen; it seemed too impossible. But the idea was appealing.

Later that year, I received a wire from Stravinsky: "I'm writing something for you. It will be my Christmas present to you and the band."

It was one of the wildest psychological moments I ever had. Having one of the world's great composers write for me was beyond imagination.

Then Stravinsky's lawyer called Goldfarb and said, "Do you realize that Stravinsky can't afford to live, let alone be giving away music?" So we arranged to get him a fee.

Stravinsky was living in California, not far from me in Hollywood. When I met him, I found a wonderful man with a great sense of humor. We spent hours just talking about everything but music. He was amusing and amazing. His English was good, but heavily accented, and he pronounced my name more as Wood-He than Woody.

Much later, during an evening at my home, I asked him, "Mr. Stravinsky, you must tell me about French clarinetists, about German clarinetists, and the difference in their performance."

He replied, "French clarinet players: very good technique, quick tongue, very small sounds. The German players: technique not so good, tongue not so good, but very big sound . . . But you, Woody . . . Ah!"

I could have kissed him.

About Christmastime, he came to New York to rehearse the band for "Ebony Concerto." We were playing the Paramount Theater, doing six or seven shows a day, and we used a rehearsal hall upstairs. We had about an hour and twenty minutes between performances. Our brass players were all Stravinsky fans and they had been talking for days about meeting him.

The first rehearsal occurred in the morning, after the first show of the day. All the guys rushed upstairs, still wearing their uniforms—dark suits, white shirts and ties. Stravinsky arrived with a towel around his neck, wearing an old sweatshirt, grey slacks, and tennis shoes.

The rehearsal was difficult. Most of us had never received any classical training. We had to learn from each other. We fought and perspired our way through the first hour. Our nerves were completely wrenched and some of us were ready to give up. Stravinsky, sensing our collective anxiety, walked over and put his arm around me.

"Woody," he said, "you have a lovely family."

That helped reduce the pressure. We relaxed somewhat but worked like mad during the next few days.

He hummed and whistled and tapped his foot while he dragged us through it. He was only interested in whether we got it, not how we got it. It was as big a challenge for him as it was for us because he had to write out the concerto in 4/4 time. It was difficult for us to imagine, but a simple time signature like 4/4 was giving a master trouble. He told me it was torture for him, but he had to do it if he was going to write for jazz musicians.

He couldn't stay to conduct the premiere of "Ebony Concerto" in March 1946 at Carnegie Hall because of a tour that was set for him in Europe. He said he didn't care about the tour, but he had to do it to eat.

After the debut, the idea was sold as a concert and we began a tour with it across the country. Between the good receptions, there were some wacky disappointments, mainly because the tour wasn't always promoted properly. The first place we played was a hall in Baltimore. Stravinsky's protégé was conducting, and he was thrilled to death. But when we started to play the piece, the audience began to boo. They didn't want to hear it.

The concert was booked into universities, where agents figured there would be an interest in culture. Of all the schools we played, Purdue gave us the worst reception. The campus theater, which presented mostly vaudeville and show biz events, was packed. But "Ebony Concerto" thoroughly confused the audience. It was a Mexican standoff. No matter when we performed the piece—at the start of a concert, in the middle or at the finish—many of the audiences decided that the music wasn't me, that we were insulting their intelligence.

Benny Goodman, among others, was puzzled about why

Stravinsky would write a piece for me. One night I ran into him on Broadway at four in the morning, and he said, "Hey, kid, is that a hard part, that Stravinsky piece?"

"Is it hard?" I said. "Man, it's impossible."

"Oh, it can't be that hard," Benny said, making an obvious reference to how he felt about my clarinet playing.

"Listen," I said, "when I went to all the guys I could talk to at the Philharmonic and different places and had them look at it, they said, 'Jeezus, it's gonna be difficult.' "

Benny remained skeptical. "So it's a little bit difficult, but it can't be *that* hard."

I got hold of a mini-score of the concerto and sent it to his house. About six weeks later, I ran into Benny again, and he said, "Hey, that *is* a hard piece!"

From Benny, that was a big statement. He eventually did the concerto for Columbia, after we recorded it with Stravinsky conducting.

Benny had a very nutty attitude about lots of things, but it had nothing to do with his musical abilities. He was the head and shoulders of the clarinet.

We hung out socially a little bit in the forties, and once in the fifties I looked him up in Nashville after someone pointed out that he was in town. We made arrangements to meet for dinner, and I told him about a good place out in the country. But first I went to his hotel room with a bottle of gin and some vermouth. I fixed a pitcher of martinis and iced them down well.

"Hey, what's this?" Benny asked after taking a sip.

I couldn't believe he had never tried a martini. I told him what it was, and he knocked the rest of it right down. I explained that this was just a quick drink before dinner, but we wound up polishing off much of the bottle.

We never made it to the country restaurant. Instead, we held each other up and staggered into a greasy spoon across from his hotel.

10
THE HOMEFRONT

The band grossed more than a million dollars in 1946, and Charlotte and I were anxious to invest some of our earnings in a home. We moved early in 1946 to Laurel Canyon, where we leased a place for a few months while we were looking.

The house we fell in love with was being vacated by Humphrey Bogart and Lauren Bacall. It was high on Hollywood Boulevard, with a sweeping view of the valley from a large rear terrace which jutted out from the mountainside at the center level of the three stories.

Bacall was the businessperson in that real estate deal, and a pain in the ass, too.

We bought the house for about $60,000 cash, and things couldn't have seemed rosier. The band was riding high, the family was ensconced in the Hollywood Hills, and we had such sociable neighbors as Robert Benchley and Charlie Butterworth.

Beneath the surface, however, a major problem was growing. It had begun to develop a couple of years earlier, when we were living at the Garden of Allah complex. Charlotte had begun drinking and she was taking pills. As I told Gene Lees much later, you start mixing Nembutals with booze, and you're on your way home.

I suppose she was influenced by the movie crowd who lived there, and my absence for up to forty weeks a year on the road contributed to her difficulty.

I was disturbed about it, but there wasn't a great deal I could do. Like anyone with a drinking problem, she had many excuses. I even threatened to take a walk. But it was an empty gesture; we were very tight.

Charlotte suffered greatly and really tried to beat the rap. Eventually, she sought psychiatrists and other help by herself. One of the more drastic steps she took was to undergo shock treatments. Ingrid, meanwhile, was always well taken care of by Charlotte and a live-in nursemaid.

I talked to my close friends about the problem—Jack Siefert in Philadelphia, Ray Sherman and his wife in Milwaukee, and Don and Elsa Cummings. Don was a comic and Elsa had been very close to Charlotte since the early days when they had danced in shows together.

I decided that the only way I could help was to go home.

So I broke up the band.

It was just before the Christmas holidays in 1946, and I handled it with the guys as well as I could. I told them that I thought we had gone as far as we were going with the band, and I gave them sufficient notice.

I went to Alcoholics Anonymous meetings with Charlotte, to keep her company, and, the first time we arrived at one, I saw a lot of my ex-band members and many of my friends. I remember Billy May greeting me with open arms, and I told him: "I'm cool, you know. I'm just here with Charlotte." I enjoyed the meetings. It was nice to hear people bare their souls.

Being off the road was a situation I hadn't known since I was eight. It was appealing to eat dinner with my family, play with my daughter—carrying on with her out in the yard and throwing her into the bathtub.

I did a California radio show once a week with Peggy Lee and her husband, Dave Barbour, who led the band. I didn't want to be a bandleader. I was just the boy singer with Peggy. It worked out fine.

Ralph Burns put together a band, and I sang some tunes with them. I was invited to do a radio deejay show, on which we would play new releases and judge them. It was beautiful because we'd get angry phone calls.

I opened an office in what was probably the most auspicious location in the Wilshire district of Los Angeles: the former offices of Robbins Music in the Beverly Wilshire Hotel. It was on the mezzanine, which led to the outdoor pool. Anyone who wanted to reach my office was usually connected to the bar at poolside. It was a classy operation.

I installed a couple of my former road managers in that office: Jack Archer, who had worked for the band in the late thirties before marrying our female trumpet player, Billy Rogers, and leaving to start their own group; and Milton Deutsch, who had replaced Archer. With them I had Abe Turchen, who was road manager before I folded the First Herd.

Among the things they decided to do was to handle bookings for a guy named Spade Cooley, who was leading a hot so-called Western swing band in California. I knew Spade casually, and I interceded for Abe and Milton, talking him into going on the road for one-nighters. He had never done that before. He was a Los Angeles product with some minor league hits on the Victor label, and he had stuck to his home base.

Spade Cooley consented, and I advised the guys in my office: "Take him up and down the West Coast and back again. And don't go any farther east than Nevada. Anywhere else, they're not going to know him." It worked like a charm. They got good guarantees and they hit percentages every night.

They thought the boat had come in and decided to be courageous. They took him into Iowa and the surrounding area with a complete revue—horses, dancers, singers, a show biz thing. Nobody knew him, or cared, and I started to get phone calls at four in the morning. It was Spade Cooley, making soulful, moaning sounds such as, "Like, man, I'm ruined." It was a terrible fiasco. I think he had to walk back halfway to the coast.

My office quietly dissolved. Cooley wound up in jail many years later on a murder conviction.

I had fun for seven months without any urge to get back in front of a band.

11
THE SECOND HERD

One night, some friends and I went out to a little joint on Sunset near Vine Street. Phil Moore, a pianist and arranger, was leading a little group there that included trumpeter Ernie Royal and his brother, Marshall Royal, who later joined Count Basie.

When I heard Ernie play so fluently at the top of the horn, it gave me the hots for music again. Trying to make something different happen was always in the back of my mind. You hear a great player or two and the idea is replanted, as long as I could do it without having to return to what I already did.

The family problems were taken care of, and I felt I had to do something productive again.

Jimmy Giuffre, hearing that I might be organizing a band, told me he had an idea for a different saxophone sound. We started sending for guys. Most of them were at the beach, just bumming around, including Zoot Sims and Stan Getz. We sent to Boston for Serge Chaloff, because we wanted a dancer in the band. He had already fooled around with the Jimmy Dorsey band, and somebody who had heard him said, "This guy's far out." He was.

As we put together a roster of players, I kept wondering how far I could go with this new bebop sound. My fear was that we would not be able to top ourselves, that we would reach the end of the rope. I didn't want to go backwards, repeating what I had already done. When that happens, the music just becomes repetition, which is what most bands were about. I never felt that way with the First Herd.

I never wanted to sell nostalgia. Where there are certain tunes closely associated with the band, it would be unfair not to play a few on occasion to recapture memories for people. But I never considered it our big job, or our future, to delve further into the past.

Holdovers from the First Herd included Shorty Rogers on trumpet, Sam Marowitz on alto sax, and Don Lamond on drums. Walt Yoder, who had been at the core of the original Band That Plays the Blues, returned as our bassist. Along with Rogers, our writers were Ralph Burns, Jimmy Giuffre, Al Cohn, and John LaPorta.

A bandful of young, sharp players filled the rest of the lineup. With Rogers and Royal, the trumpet section held Stan Fishelson, Bernie Glow, and Marky Markowitz. Earl Swope buoyed the trombone section, with Ollie Wilson and Bob Swift. Gene Sargent played guitar, Jerry Ney doubled on vocals and vibes, and Fred Otis was the pianist.

The Second Herd was launched on the evening of October 16, 1947, at Municipal Auditorium, in San Bernardino, California.

The centerpiece of the band was the three-tenor-and-a-baritone sax section, a configuration that I kept with every big band that followed. Its anthem was Jimmy Giuffre's "Four Brothers," which soon became the band's subtitle. Giuffre's tune helped to set a style for the band. The original Four Brothers were Zoot Sims, Stan Getz, and Herbie Steward on tenors and Serge Chaloff on baritone. The sequence of sax solos on the original recording, by the way, was Zoot, Serge, Herbie, and Stan.

The Second Herd was organized with the full intent of going straight ahead with bebop. Ralph Burns and Shorty Rogers were still writing some of our arrangements, but the bebop evolution had become the core of our music. We gathered invention and diversification not only from the charts of Al Cohn and Jimmy Giuffre, but from the provocative, emotional sounds of our reed and brass soloists. After a few months, Al Cohn replaced Herbie Steward as a member of the Four Brothers, and Mary Ann McCall returned as our singer early in 1948.

Ralph Burns added a fourth movement to his "Summer Sequence," the first three parts of which we had premiered with the First Herd at Carnegie Hall, when we played "Ebony Concerto" for the first time. Ralph wrote the fourth part as an epilogue because Columbia needed more music to fill out a "Summer Sequence" album.

With a few melodic changes, the fourth part was retitled "Early Autumn," and Johnny Mercer, who was one of America's greatest poets, wrote exquisite lyrics to it. Stan Getz was the tenor soloist on the original recording, and seldom in the history of music has one record established the reputation of a player as "Summer Sequence" did for Stan. But also listen to the trombone playing of Ollie Wilson on that cut. I always thought he showed a lot of promise. And Ralph plays super piano on all four segments of "Summer Sequence."

Shorty Rogers, who helped with a lot of things in the First

Herd, was writing terrific bebop charts. He was one of the great contributors to both bands. Red Norvo, who was his brother-in-law then, was helpful in bringing him to us.

Don Lamond was playing drums, and he made that rhythm section. We had some changes in the other spots, but once it settled in, it was great. Chubby Jackson even returned after a while.

Lamond recalls:

The Four Brothers band was the best band. Maybe it wasn't quite as fiery as the First Herd, with "Caldonia" and "Apple Honey" and all. But it was the best.

The band was spectacular. But the public wasn't ready for it. Unlike the previous herd, it wasn't playing the pop music of the day.

We were getting some terrific receptions on tour, but we weren't getting enough bookings. We moved from Columbia to Capitol because Carlos Gastel, who was handling our personal management, felt he could pull some weight there. Other artists he handled, such as Peggy Lee and Nat Cole, were also recording for Capitol. But we weren't selling records like we had in the early forties. Even Sinatra had pretty much cooled off during that period.

The band's downfall was caused by a combination of things. But changing the sound was certainly a big factor. It was something I felt I had to do. The audience that could understand "Apple Honey," however, couldn't relate to "Lemon Drop" or "Four Brothers." Musically, the bebop route was magnificent. But business-wise, it was the dumbest thing I ever did. Those pieces didn't really succeed, except with a small percentage of our listeners, until the mid-1950s. If we had just continued playing "Apple Honey" and "Caldonia," we'd probably have had a fighting chance.

The band was an albatross. The first year of its operation cost me $175,000, which I didn't have. In order to keep refinancing it, I used the side-door method—doing brief tours with a small group. I would take out a sextet for a trip to keep my feet on the ground with a little profit.

Among those who came through that band at one time or another were bassist Oscar Pettiford and drummers Shadow Wilson and Shelly Manne. Replacements in the sax section included Jimmy Giuffre, Gene Ammons, and Billy Mitchell. Red Rodney joined the trumpet section in the fall of 1948.

Red Rodney recalls:

I took the place of Marky Markowitz when the band was at the Royal Roost in New York City. Chubby Jackson had called me to join when the band was being organized, but I couldn't make it. I told him I wasn't interested then in going with a big band. I was getting my feet wet on 52nd Street, and I had just been with Claude Thornhill and I wanted to be in a small band. The only reason I joined in 1948 was I needed a job; I needed the money. Woody offered good money and being with that band was an opportunity to help my career. I know that everyone says it was a financial flop, but musically it was Number One. It was the hippest and the best.

The First Herd was a unique band; it was different. But it wasn't rated by the jazz musicians as well as the Second Herd. Ours was much more musical, more subtle. Al Cohn was writing for us and Shorty Rogers, and of course Ralph Burns. He was the head writer; they all learned a great deal from him.

I had the fifth trumpet chair, which was the solo chair. Shorty, who was a soloist also, would write all the solos on my chair. I even said to him, "Shorty, why do you do this?" I was embarrassed. And he said, "Because this will be very good for you." Shorty is an unselfish guy. He really tried to make me shine. Bernie Glow was the relief lead trumpet. Stan Fishelson was the lead. Ernie Royal was the high lead. He did it beautifully. It was a dynamite band. I got a lot to play in the band. Shorty and I were the two bebop trumpet players, he the more subtle one and I the more fiery one. Woody certainly featured Ernie Royal a lot, and Ernie did a lot for that band.

Although I wasn't floored by the band when I joined, I became thrilled with it after I got there. I was really a young bebopper. I was known on 52nd Street. That was for me. But I really enjoyed playing with that big band and traveling with the guys. The adults were Bill Harris and Sam Marowitz. The rest of us were kids.

Don Lamond was our age, but he was more adult. Serge Chaloff was my roommate. He was the character of the band. Everybody was friends. We had fights among ourselves, but if anybody else was fighting us, we protected each other.

I would say that a good thirty percent of the book was modern bebop charts. A lot of times they were flexible; you could open them up. And guys would make their own backup, especially the saxophone section.

Soloist-wise, Serge and I were the two beboppers. Of course, you couldn't say that Al, Zoot, and Stan were bebop players; they were more modern versions of Lester Young.

We had all kinds of flexibility in the arrangements. Not on the ones that Ralph Burns did; he would hate when we would do it to him. He wanted everything as he had written it. But Shorty Rogers loved it. It would help him learn how to write; he used it as a vehicle for learning.

Woody was very smart to have guys in the band write for the band, because a guy writing in the band knows exactly what everybody can do and what's best for them. Shorty and Al Cohn would not write first trumpet, second trumpet, and so on. They would write Ernie, Fish, Ray. They knew which person they wanted to play each part.

It was a tremendous part of my early learning experience. It helped me learn the subtleties.

Al Cohn loved Woody. But it took a while for Woody to like him. He had Zoot and Stan, and all of a sudden Al comes in who was not as flamboyant as either of the other two. But musically, every time Al played a solo, the trumpet section and the trombone section would lean forward to listen. It didn't take Woody long to recognize Al's greatness.

Chubby knew Woody better than anybody. They were personal friends and musical buddies from the same era, the same idiom. Chubby had been part of Woody's greatest triumphs, and Woody was much more comfortable with that "Apple Honey" band than he ever was with the "Four Brothers" band. But to his credit, he knew how great that "Four Brothers" band was.

When I got there, Al was still there, but Zoot and Stan were gone. Gene Ammons came in. Shadow Wilson was there on drums, but he lasted only a second; he couldn't play. Woody gave him plenty of opportunity, and it didn't work.

Then Shelly Manne came in, and we all looked at him as a Stan Kenton drummer. We hated Stan Kenton. Don't forget, we were kids then. Today we wouldn't look at it like that. Shelly sat down and played that book from the very first note. All of us went over and hugged him and told him how great he was.

Woody must be given a lot of credit, coming out of the swing era, for putting together and keeping together that band, and getting the best out of each guy.

He was a sensitive man, and everybody loved him.

I solved the problem of being away from my family by bringing them along when I played somewhere interesting, even if it was far from home. If we were performing at a theater in New York, Charlotte and Ingrid would be backstage, talking to the people we were working with. Later, in 1955, the two of them traveled to Europe with the band.

The big band period was over. That's why all those guys who led big dance bands took their umbrellas and ran. Only the jazz bands with the nitty gritty remained—us, Duke Ellington, Count Basie. Everybody else ran for cover. Louis Armstrong went to the All-Star sextet format.

I knew Louis very well. Joe Glazer, his manager, told Abe Turchen, "I'm going to bastardize my artist," meaning Louis, "and put him on a tour with Woody's band." We did long tours on a bill with his All-Star group.

Louis was a good friend. He had all the charm, even though he felt that what he was doing then was a mere shadow of himself. You still had to give him credit because he could pull it off.

Jack Siefert recalls:

Woody had been fond of Louis Armstrong since childhood. One of his treasured possessions was Louis's recording of "Struttin' with Some Barbecue." In 1980, when Woody became the first white man to be honored and crowned as King of the Zulus at the Mardi Gras in New Orleans, he featured that tune.

When Woody and Louis were doing their tour together, Woody purchased a couple of beautiful white silk ties for Louis that would go well with his famed white handkerchief. Louis was thrilled. He thanked Woody warmly and said, "Do me a favor, Woody, and autograph these ties."

Woody just broke up.

When Louis passed away, Woody was visiting us at the Jersey shore. He received a call about the death and was asked to be an honorary pallbearer.

The band business in general had taken quite a nose dive. The future was easily foreseen, if you were alert and paid attention. But I nonetheless reinvested practically whatever money we were able to put together into the 1948 and '49 band. I felt strongly about the music we were playing and I couldn't accept the fact that we didn't have a wider audience. When I found that I was $175,000 in the hole, I became very much aware.

We rapidly lost the audience that had been ours during the First Herd. And I no longer wanted to play nursemaid to the players who were on narcotics.

12
HORSE PLAY

It was no secret that we had quite a few junkies in the Second Herd. It never became a serious problem on the bandstand, although sometimes guys missed a bus or otherwise had trouble getting to a gig on time. But the drugs didn't appear to cut into their musical ability, which is why I put up with it as long as I did.

I was so naïve about it at the beginning that I didn't know why guys were nodding out on the bandstand. On the bus, the guys who were hooked sat in a section of their own. Serge Chaloff would hang a blanket to separate his group from the rest of the band and would distribute the goodies.

My difficulties with Serge's behavior led to a confrontation in Washington, D.C. I told the story to Gene Lees, and he set down the details in his *Jazzletter*.

Gene Lees recalls:

The band not only looked bad, it sounded bad. Woody, furious at what had happened to it, had a row right on the bandstand with "Mr. Chaloff," as he called him, emphasis on the first syllable.

"He was getting farther and farther out there," Woody said. "He kept saying, 'Hey, Woody, baby, I'm straight, man, I'm clean.' And I shouted, 'Just play your goddamn part and shut up!'

"I was so depressed after that gig. There was this after-hours joint in Washington called the Turf and Grid. It was owned by a couple of guys with connections, bookmakers. Numbers guys. Everybody used to go there. That night President Truman had a party at the White House, and afterward all his guests went over to the Turf and Grid. They were seven deep at the bar, and I had to fight my way through to get a drink, man. All I wanted was to have a drink and forget it. And finally I get a couple of drinks, and it's hot in there, and I'm sweating, and somebody's got their hands on me, and I hear, 'Hey Woody, baby, whadya wanna talk to me like that for? I'm straight, baby, I'm straight.' And it's Mr. Chaloff. And then I remember an old Joe Venuti bit. We were jammed in there, packed in, and . . . I peed down Serge's leg.

"You know, man, when you do that to someone, it takes a while before it sinks in what's happened to him. And when Serge realized, he let out a howl like a banshee. He pushed out through the crowd and went into a telephone booth. And I'm banging on the door and trying to get at him, and one of the owners comes up and says, 'Hey, Woody, you know we love you, and we love the band, but we can't have you doing things like that in here.' And he asked me to please cool it.

"Well, not long after that, I was back here on the [West] Coast, working at some club at the beach. Joe Venuti was playing just down the street, and I was walking on the beach with him after the gig one night, and I told him I had a confession to make. I'd stolen one of his bits. I told him about peeing on Serge's leg, and Joe just about went into shock. He was horrified. He said, 'Woody, you can't do things like that! I can do things like that, but you can't! You're a gentleman. It's all right for me, but not you!' "

As far as their musicianship was concerned, there was no

trouble at all. But it really never affected the music or our performances. They were all excellent players. But the health of some individuals was in pitiful order. And the health problem was growing.

There was a great exaggeration of how many guys were deeply involved. But it was bad enough that we lost one or two of them, and at an early age. That was heartbreak enough—Sonny Berman and later Serge Chaloff. A couple of others were borderline cases, but fortunately some people are physically or mentally stronger.

The players in my band were pretty open to me about it. One young trumpet player from New York, Bernie Glow, confessed everything to me. But he was proud that he could handle it. When his mother and father finally got wise to him and sent him to their physician, the report was that Bernie was a twenty-one-year-old who had the body of a sixty-year-old man. He went on a long health kick and beat the rap.

A number of others recovered, including Al Cohn, Zoot Sims, and Stan Getz.

I had no personal knowledge of the actual extent of anyone's habit, such as how many things someone needed every day. That wasn't my concern, and I didn't feel I had a right to know, or enough knowledge to advise them properly.

I had tried pot as a kid, but I never liked it. When I was a sophomore in high school, about 1929, I joined a band and spent part of that summer in Tulsa, Oklahoma, where we played in a kind of auditorium that held several hundred high school teenagers. The girls were known as pigs and the boys were known as toads. Immediately, when a dance ended, they would run out into the oil fields, listen to the oil pumps and the drills make all the wild sounds, and pass a little joint, a stick of marijuana. It was universal among a great deal of high school kids in that area.

But with some guys, if grass made them feel pretty good,

they wanted something that made them feel a little bit better. It's always a big shock to them when they find they have a big, fancy, expensive habit. Early in the days of bebop, there was peer pressure. A lot of players who wanted to play in the top echelon thought there was a connection with drugs.

It was never proven. The guys who could play great could do it whether or not they were stoned. And many of them, including Charlie Parker, admitted that their playing was often inferior when they were high.

I think they also were drawn into the bag because the salesmen were out there greeting them, like it was the natural thing to do. I saw a lot of it, the connections. I was well aware of it. I saw the guys out there trying to score. But I remained the biggest square in life.

Some of the players used the difficulty of the road life as an excuse for drugs. But I don't think the road had a fucking thing to do with it. They just wanted to get high, and the contacts were everywhere, and still are. If a guy wants anything, he can get it anywhere at any time of the day or night.

Mental strain has nothing to do with it, either. The worst strain is when a guy decides to become a family person. And those guys rarely got into drugs.

Red Rodney recalls:

We were good kids even though we were doing bad things. I must clarify that. Everybody knows there was a lot of junk in that band. I was not using junk at that time. I didn't start until later. Nobody believes that to this day, because it turns out I was the more famous junky of all of them, because I continued, and I got caught a little more. With that band, however, I smoked pot, but I did not use junk.

Every once in a while, Woody would get on the bus and say, "Fellas, I got a tip that they're waiting for us in the next town." I don't think he was lying. Serge Chaloff did get busted once. But Woody got him out.

I was horrified by what these guys were doing. And all of a sudden, we became neurotic. Guys were strung out, there was no good morning, there was no high, there was no happiness. Everybody was bugged. I saw that happening.

I was concerned about the drug problem, but my overriding focus was to produce good music. I think a great deal of the music we set down for posterity at that time still lives very well today in the state in which it was put together. I found that if the players were well enough, they played extremely well. If they weren't well enough, they played adequately.

I don't think anyone ever accomplished or proved anything by saying, "You're involved in narcotics, get out of my band." If a person has ability, he must have a chance to show his ability. But I think that every young man in the band at that time, and anytime before and since, was very much aware that I didn't approve of narcotics of any kind.

The only other bandleader whose opinion I took stock in was Duke Ellington, who had some major druggies in his band as well. Duke thought pretty much like I did. "If the players could play, let 'em play." He didn't try to change them or fix them or anything else.

Chubby Jackson recalls:

Woody never did any drugs, I can attest to that. He got into his drinking and he smoked cigarettes a lot. He even quit drinking for a while. But after a while, trying to relate every night to guys coming up to him saying, "Hey man, what's happening," he would do, "Hey man, see you later." And he'd go to the bar. On the road, he rarely had anyone to talk to. It's "Hey, Woody, sign this for my sister Adrienne," and "How do you like it here in Vero Beach." His retorts got a little satirical; there was a little edge on them.

I drank whiskey, but I never felt it had me even close to whipped. There were periods when I went on the wagon or cut my intake. In the 1950s, I went down to beer. I couldn't drink that much beer, and I think it helped me. Eventually, I started feeling better. But I finally turned back to whiskey.

Alcohol was Doctor Feelgood's tonic.

George Simon recalls:

Woody and I were good friends, but I always had a feeling that he thought I was a goody-goody-two-shoes because I didn't drink. I hate the taste of it. Also it slows me down and I don't have as much fun. Woody used to kid me about it.

In the early days, I saw him and Charlotte socially. And he used to visit us in Stamford, Connecticut, in the early fifties. It was always a very warm relationship.

When the band was playing at the Cafe Rouge in the Hotel Pennsylvania, in about 1945, a waiter came over one evening and served me the most god-awful concoction of ice cream and things, from Woody.

We kept trying to make a go of the Second Herd. But it appeared that the ballgame was over, not only for us, but for big bands in general.

13
END OF
AN ERA

Several things contributed to the end of the big band era, but the most obvious was that the war hysteria had come to a close, and the emphasis shifted. The public was listening to singers rather than commercial dance bands. And simple economics had reduced the size of jazz bands, which no longer were playing the popular music of the day.

Few of the Swing Era bands, of course, ever played jazz. For each Duke Ellington, there were a hundred Mickey Mouse stylistic bands. During the height of that period, we were competing primarily with Duke, Count Basie, Benny Goodman, Charlie Barnet, Chick Webb, Andy Kirk, Jimmy Lunceford, and the Dorseys.

Sammy Kaye, on the other hand, was one of my top

choices for a band with no music. Kay Kyser was a very good showman, but his bands were contrived.

I knew Basie pretty well, but we weren't buddy-buddy. Sometimes we'd have a drink together, and once he came to my house for dinner with Joe Williams in the fifties. That was one of the very high periods for the Basie band.

I became good friends with Duke while we were both recording for Columbia, where they thought it would be a good idea if I did two vocal sides with him. I remember getting a call from Columbia to meet with Duke to work out the keys. I said, sure, and I went into Hollywood, around Vine Street, where Duke was staying. I picked him up to take him to my house, and he said he had to be back in an hour or so.

"Don't worry about it," I said. "I'll get you back."

So we drove up to my house, which hangs down a mountain and has a fantastic view of the city. We walked into the living room and Duke looked out and said, "My God, it's beautiful."

Then I remembered that he liked ice cream, and I got some out of the freezer and laid it on him. He had to be back in an hour, and he stayed for two days.

Charlie Barnet and I weren't peas of the same pod. He was a wealthy man's son and I was a struggling guy in another world, but we were friends.

Artie Shaw was probably the world's greatest natural clarinetist. He had impossible range and could play anything. But he suffered from other things. He felt it was beneath his dignity to have to sign autographs and play for dancers. He saw it as a horrible way to go through life, so he just took a walk.

I didn't feel either way about the dancers, but I was continually amazed by how few people can keep time. Standing on the stage and trying to swing, and being an ex-hoofer, it would drive me crazy to watch their feet. And when they complained to me about the tempo, I would tell them, "I'll listen to you when you learn to dance."

I respected Glenn Miller in the early days because of his arranging ability. Claude Thornhill, too, had good taste and proved it in writing for many people. He also had the good taste to discover a great singer like Maxine Sullivan.

Of the Dorseys, I liked Jimmy best because he was easy to understand. Tommy was forceful, a businessman-operator, who used every possible device to get what he wanted. He was also an excellent, meticulous musician. Jimmy was more carefree. He had an abundance of technique but he never really concentrated on sound.

Tommy was the more successful by far, but Jimmy had proven all of his points. We were both playing at an amusement park once, when Jimmy drove over to see me in a new Cadillac convertible.

"Woody," he said, "this is what 'Amapola' gave me." He had a sense of humor. If you want to hear Tommy's sense of humor, listen to Frank Sinatra. He's a complete copy of Tommy Dorsey, including the sarcasm.

Harry James decided that if he was going to win in the big band game, he had to get a ballad sound. So he made an exaggerated vibrato and pulled it off. And poor Gene Krupa paid forever for his one stupid mistake, being caught with grass.

Among the others, Boyd Raeburn's band was preposterous, overarranged. Freddy Martin had quite a good musical group, but he was never involved in jazz. Les Brown's was a good competent dance band, without room for movement. And Frankie Carle and Vaughn Monroe led stylistic or commercial bands, not unlike Sammy Kaye's or Kay Kyser's. Even among the commercial groups, however, there was some honesty and quality. But not much jazz.

14

A NEW BEGINNING

The quality of the music alone made it difficult to throw in the towel on the Second Herd. The rhythm section, with Chubby Jackson, Lou Levy on piano, and Don Lamond was cooking, and Terry Gibbs joined us on vibes, taking the place of guitarist Jimmy Raney. The arrangements by Al Cohn, Ralph Burns, and Shorty Rogers were supplemented by new charts from Tiny Kahn and Johnny Mandel.

Pianist Lou Levy recalls:

We had a great Johnny Mandel arrangement of "What's New?" that featured vibraphone. Terry Gibbs played it, and then Bags [Milt Jackson] got to play it. Johnny also wrote an original, "Not Really the Blues," that we recorded, but it wasn't the full version because we were making 78-rpm records. It was a great piece.

There was a fierce loyalty toward the music in the band, because there were so many wonderful soloists and a wonderful ensemble. The camaraderie about the music was always obvious. There was just so much talent that something would always carry the band through. Even a mediocre night would be a great night.

During the period when Oscar Pettiford took Chubby's place and Shadow Wilson and Gene Ammons were in the band, we did a ten-week tour of Loew's theaters that began on the West Coast. A few days later, I got a communiqué saying that, when we got to the Capitol Theater in Washington, D.C., we were to abide by the contract, which stipulated that we have an entire white orchestra. "And if you do not," it went on, "the entire tour will be canceled."

Weird. Here we were, a white band except for those three players, greeted wonderfully in black theaters across the country. But in the seat of democracy, in the capital's largest theater, we're told that black players weren't welcome.

I met with the three black players and explained the problem, that they had to be replaced for this one engagement, or the entire tour would be sacrificed. I gave them their pay and expense money, and they went to New York. But they returned a day later with lawyers, demanding that the blackout be protested. I told them it was up to them; they could take the time off with pay, or leave the band. They decided to wait out the engagement and they finished the ten-week tour with us.

Milt Jackson, one of the finest musicians I ever met, took over the vibes from Terry Gibbs just as the Second Herd was winding down early in 1949.

Milt Jackson recalls:

I started with the band in about February, in Chicago, and I stayed two years. We had a very good relationship. Woody respected me as an artist, and he showed it by his treatment. I never had any problems with him.

When the band was in Chicago one time, the band had some time off before we were to play in New York. Woody and Abe Turchen were flying to New York and I mentioned that I was going to Detroit. They had bought a new car, an Oldsmobile, and Abe asked if I would drive the car to New York for him. I said I would stop in Detroit for a couple of days and then bring the car to New York. He said fine.

I went to Detroit, and the next day, on Sunday, I was taking my mother to church and a cop stopped me for some thing about the out-of-town license plates. They hadn't had time to get the plates, and they had a tag stuck on the back window. I think the car was registered in Illinois, and Abe was going to get the plates elsewhere. I don't remember what the violation was, if any.

The car was brand-new, and the cops apparently thought it was stolen. They may have imagined that I had just got it off a lot somewhere. They stopped me, and we went through this routine, and they took me down to the station. They made me take out my wallet and money, and they looked through my credentials. I had about seven hundred dollars in my pocket 'cause I had just gotten paid. That only enhanced them thinking that the car was stolen. Here he is with all this money.

I explained that part, that I played with the Woody Herman band and that I had just been paid a couple of weeks pay, and that I was home for a couple of days before driving the car back to New York for them. That made the tale even more preposterous to the cops.

So they put out all kinds of bulletins and things. I said, "To simplify things, why don't you call Woody Herman, and get him to verify this, and I'll pay for the call, if necessary." Somehow, I got them to put the call through.

I explained to Woody what had happened. Then the man took the telephone to verify if it was really Woody Herman. Woody proceeded to read him the riot act. He exploded over the phone. I could hear Woody giving him hell. Evidently, it was enough to convince them that my story was genuine. And they let me go with a tremendous apology, of course, after the delay of two or three hours. Then I drove the car to New York.

There's another interesting tale about Woody. He found out some-how about me having perfect pitch and a photographic memory. It turned into sort of a game. He would try to find some music that he thought I couldn't play or didn't know. For some reason, it got to him, and he would go to a music store, get a tune he liked and have an arrangement written up, maybe by Al Cohn or Jimmy Giuffre. And it got to be interesting, because I enjoyed the challenge.

One night he came in and said, "I got you."

"OK," I said. He had had an arrangement made up of "Stars Fell on Alabama." His theory was that I was too young to know that tune. He brought out the arrangement, and we rehearsed it. The next night we played the piece, and I had a solo on it. When I played it, he was surprised that I knew the tune. It was no problem. I explained to him that, even if it wasn't a tune I actually knew, I could play it if I heard it. Those years, I could hear any kind of a tune and im-mediately play it back. That got him, and he finally gave up. He said, "Man, I won't try that anymore."

We got to be real good friends.

"Lullabye of the Leaves" was one of the tunes that I played solo with the rhythm section often. I had fallen in love with the tune from Art Tatum, who had one of the most beautiful versions of it that I ever heard. I was drawn to it. I was playing it one night, and Woody was standing next to me. He was completely enraptured, and I noticed it. And a thought came to me.

I motioned and said, "Hey man, pick up your horn—not the clarinet, the alto." And when I finished playing my solo, he played. I never heard him so inspired. To me, the whole two years I was in the band, that was the most beautiful solo I had ever heard him play on either of those instruments. That was on the job, at a concert we were doing. He got such a kick out of it.

He told me afterward, "Man, you inspired me so tremendously." Our relationship was like that.

I became good friends with Buddy Childers, who was playing first trumpet. One night in Terre Haute, Indiana, after the gig, we were invited out to a nightclub. When we got there, they refused to let me in. One of those cases of racism.

I said, "OK, I'll go back to the hotel because I know what it's about out here. And I'm not going to make any extra waves and start any trouble."

I started to leave, and Buddy said, "Uh-uh. You came with us and you're gonna go in." He called the manager, and he said, "Hey, we were invited by your management to be guests of the nightclub, and he's one of the featured members of the band and he's with us."

Buddy was getting rather insistent. I didn't want to cause any trouble, and he told me, "Hey, man, you just stand there. Be cool. Don't worry, I got this covered." Then he turned to the manager and said, "You gonna let us in or you want some trouble?" We wound up going in.

Buddy liked to play golf, and he always kept a set of clubs in the back of the bus. One day during a real hot summer month, they couldn't get a window open in the bus. So Serge Chaloff took one of Buddy's golf clubs out of the bag to pry the window open. When Buddy discovered the bent club and found out that Serge had done it, he threatened him with physical harm. Man, they had to separate them.

I finally disbanded the Second Herd in 1949. There were no hard feelings; we all knew that the band was a financial bust, that we couldn't get enough bookings.

To try to recoup momentarily, at least, I put together a Woodchoppers septet—with Milt Jackson, Conte Candoli, guitarist Dave Barbour, bassist Red Mitchell, Bill Harris, and Shelly Manne—and went to Cuba.

Milt was especially astounding during that trip. Most of the Cubans, other than local musicians, didn't know what we were playing, so I utilized Milt's graceful vibes sound as often as I could. In one show there, I asked him to play a medley and he chose standard ballads, performing them beautifully, and we won over the crowd. I couldn't upset him with a tune.

He knew every old standard, the proper bridges and all the proper changes. He was invaluable.

Milt Jackson recalls:

We stayed in Cuba for four weeks, through Christmas and New Year's. On Christmas Eve it rained and wiped us out in the outdoor nightclub. The owner went to the hospital with a heart attack. On New Year's Eve, the same thing happened. The biggest night of their whole year. I think it sent him back to the hospital.

The audiences hadn't heard of Woody's records very much in Cuba. He wasn't that well known there. Things like "Don't Cry Joe" and "Happiness Is Just a Thing Called Joe," both of which were big hits in the States, got little applause there. People reacted very casually to them. Woody was getting sort of frustrated.

So one night I called him to the side and said, "Woody, I think I ought to make you aware of something. I think the problem is that they don't know these tunes down here."

I had a collapsible set of vibes, and we were playing a tune one night when the legs gradually began to collapse. I moved down with them and never stopped playing.

Red Mitchell recalls:

I started with Woody in Cuba, at the Tropicana, in November of 1949, and stayed with him to the beginning of 1952. He was great. Needless to say, we weren't All-Stars at the time. I found him under all circumstances to be whatever we needed. He could be a leader, he could be a brother figure, or just a friend. He was there and available.

Milt and I were rooming together in Cuba. We shared an apartment. We had cockroaches and Milt used his entire Spanish vocabulary telling the owner about the cucarachas. The owner just laughed. One day we got all the poison we could buy, sprays and all, and did up the apartment. When we came back, the place was crawling with dying cockroaches. I put as many as possible out of their misery.

He had that small group for four months, and that was fun. After Cuba, we went to Philadelphia. Then we played northward, and I remember that everyplace we went it was twenty degrees colder. Then we went to the Midwest and to Texas and to California. It was a nice tour.

I remember a scene in Indiana, where we worked a ballroom of a hotel, and after the gig we went into the coffee shop to eat. The manager came over to us and said, "The boy will have to eat upstairs." We looked at him and said, "There's no boys here, we're all men. What do you mean?"

"Well, you know," he said.

Milt tried to be as graceful about it as he could. The rest of us ordered food and sent it back; ordered it again and sent it back again. The third time it came, we all got up and walked out, getting glares from the kitchen.

From California, we went back to New York and Woody reformed the big band. He wanted to have a clean big band this time. He had Ralph Burns rewrite the book. We played the Capitol Theater for a month. I remember Bill Farrell had a written routine. He was a former bass player turned singer, and he was the first singer I ever worked with. He had it written into his act that he tore up his tie at a certain point. He had certain lines, whether they worked or not. The funny part about that was they didn't work.

Gene Baylos was on the bill, and all the comedians came in to hear him. And Bill Farrell, at one point in the show, would say, "That tune happens to be on my latest record, and if you'd like a copy I just happen to have a million of them in my attic." And there would always be a long silence. He never got a laugh on that line. The next tune started with an introduction where I had to use the bow. So one time I bought caps that, put under your foot, would go off. And I put two big fat caps on the floor. When he said that line about the tune and his record, there was a long silence and—BAM! BAM!—I think Woody knew who did it. I don't think it increased his affection for me. The stage manager was running back and forth behind the stage.

After that, we did a long tour of one-nighters. The band was all white then, and we played all-white places or, a couple of times, all-black places. I remember once we played an all-white place and one of *the customers came up and liked the band, and wanted to pay me a compliment. He was shuffling his feet and looking at the floor. He wanted to tell me he liked my playing and he liked the way the band sounded, and I couldn't catch his eye. I kept ducking and trying to catch his eye. I thought to myself, Damn, this guy's sick. It's gonna be a long time before this thing heals.*

At one place, we played a white-on-white country club outside of Birmingham, Alabama. During one of the intermissions, the lady that had hired the band, the social director I guess, came up to Woody while I happened to be talking to him.

She said [in a broad Southern accent], "Mistah Herman. I just want y'all to know that I think that all the things the people are saying about the band certainly are not true. I think you're doin' a fahn job."

Talk about left-handed compliments. There was nothing worse than a white nigger. We were traitors.

Every night during that tour, people would holler, "Play Dixie." At the beginning, Woody thought they meant Dixieland. He would call down a trumpet player and a trombonist and he would play "Muskrat Ramble" or something. That wasn't what they wanted to hear. It laid an egg. Then we played "Caldonia," and they didn't get that either.

I was experimenting with the amplification of the bass, as I had from the beginning. At that point I had my own microphone sitting in front of the bass on a short stand and an amplifier on the other side of the stand. They made bass pickups at that point, but I had tried them and found fault with them. This I thought was going to be more realistic. It wasn't, it turned out. Anyway, one night between tunes, I plucked out the tune "Dixie" on the bass. And the place went wild. Woody slapped his forehead, and said, "Oh, that's what they want. Well, OK."

From then on, every night "Dixie" replaced the "Caldonia" medley as the climax of the evening. The people would give rebel yells and holler and jump up and down, and go crazy. Every night. The whole band played it in unison.

One night—and I have to give Dave McKenna some of the credit for this, because he dared me to do it—after the cheers were dying down for "Dixie," I leaned down into my microphone, and gave a long, loud Bronx cheer. There was a hush over the whole place. A lot of people didn't realize where it was coming from. But Woody did. I had never seen him like that before. He came over to me with his head literally shaking and his eyes bugging out, and he said to me in a stage whisper, "Leave the stand."

I left the stand. They only had a few tunes left, and I think they shortened the set a little bit. I found a neutral corner. Everybody was kind of looking at everybody else. We were out of there in a flash, and Woody said to me, "Do you know you could have gotten us all lynched?"

I said, "I'm sorry. I goofed."

"Goofed!" he said. "You're less than a person," which is one of the worst things anybody's ever said to me.

You never saw a big band get out of a place so fast.

Woody could be a leader on occasion, but he was more of a catalyst. He could have made a living as just a talent scout, if he had never done anything else. He always had a way of finding talent and songs while the talent was still young enough to have to go out on the road and work. We all needed leadership now and then, and he never over-did it.

On new charts, he usually had a way of opening up a solo space or whatever was required. We used to love his clarinet playing. The rhythm section used to lay for his clarinet solos. We loved it because it would be swinging, it would be on time and in tune, and the rhythm section would come together. I loved his alto playing, too.

15
THE
THIRD HERD

Music was still the only business I knew, and I regrouped a 16-piece band in a matter of weeks, retaining a few guys from the previous band—Dave McKenna, Red Mitchell, and Milt Jackson. We moved from Columbia to MGM Records.

Howie Richmond, who had done some publicity for me, came up with an idea to help us and himself. He saw the band as a great source of new material for his growing music publishing business. He was starting a new record label, called Mars, for which we began to record. One of our first releases on that label was an instrumental called "Men From Mars."

Richmond was naturally interested in finding new material to publish, and he figured we'd be a great source for that. With the recording push from Mars, business was picking up somewhat, but the fifties wasn't a good period. Even Count Basie had temporarily cashed in the big band and was touring with a small group.

The pop market was rapidly changing because of people like Mitch Miller, who was running things at Columbia, feeding the nation sing-a-long recordings. He may have set the music business back forty years. For a legitimate oboe player, he sure caused a lot of turmoil. If he had kept playing oboe, we all would have been better off.

Milt Jackson left us, returning to Dizzy Gillespie's band. But in the constant turnover that had always been part of the big band business, we caught some new winners, such as trombonists Carl Fontana and Urbie Green. One person who was fairly undiscovered in our band was saxophonist Bill Perkins, who did another "Early Autumn" with us. He played beautifully, but his rendition would always be compared with the first one by Stan Getz. Urbie Green, too, was there during a not-important time for the band. That he became known at all is a testament to his talent.

Shorty Rogers and Chubby Jackson came again and went. So did Bill Harris and Al Cohn. We were trying to hit with anything we could, and one of Al's pieces for the band was called "Music for Dancing." Even Ernie Royal rejoined us for a while, and at one point we had Kai Winding and Frank Rehak in the trombone section.

We were in there punching, but we weren't doing much better than before. We had more buyers, because we were more dependable for them; our music wasn't as flagrantly "outside" the mainstream as the Four Brothers band. We got television shots, including the Ed Sullivan show. When we appeared on "We, the People," Shorty Rogers wrote something called "We, the People Bop."

We had one, two, or more great players in every formation of every band. I tried always to get the best players with the money we had to offer, and at one moment or another in the fifties, we attracted Al Porcino, Bill Berry, and Don Fagerquist on trumpets, Wayne Andre on trombone, drummers Sonny Igoe and Chuck Flores, and bassist Red Kelly, among others.

Constant personnel changes are taken for granted in a big band. But that fact doesn't make it any easier. It's like being married and divorced a thousand times. Every two minutes there's another tenor player in the band. You break your ass and a great trombone player is leaving because his sister is having a baby.

But there's a plus side, too. To have a successful road band requires energy—the kind you get from talented young guys. They're ambitious, and they come to you with the hope that this will be the best band they ever get a chance to play with. Some stay a few weeks, most of them stay a couple of years or so, and some stay longer because they find there's something there that can't be gotten somewhere else. Not just a steady job, but being able to play music that you can hold up your head about.

Mixed in among our strong suits were some players who didn't quite measure up. But we came out with our heads up most of the time. And, of course, weaker players often play better when they perform with better players.

New musicians didn't audition. They merely joined the band when they were needed. The system worked since the recruiting network was composed of recommendations by band members or former sidemen. I've always been proud of my association with musicians because I always had a pretty good club membership with my ex-players anywhere in the world. We always hung out first class, enjoying each other, reminiscing and carrying on like idiots. What came through generally was that the best years of their lives were with the band, when it was hard and we were scuffling. They came to realize what a ball that was, when we were playing what we

Top: Woody (left front) as a child performer in Milwaukee.

Right: Woody at age eleven in the uniform he wore for a performance of NOLA at the Wisconsin Theater.

Top left: As a teen, Woody had already begun thinking about leading a band.

Top right: The marquee of the Oshkosh Theater in Milwaukee heralding the "Boy Wonder."

Below: Promotional poster for the Tom Gerun band in 1932 featured a clowning Woody (before he changed the spelling from Woodie) and Al Morris, the singer-saxophonist who later changed his name to Tony Martin.

Left: With his tenor sax while a member of the Gus Arnheim Orchestra in late 1934. *Maurice Seymour*

Below: Posing with his bandleader, Isham Jones, in 1935. *Progress*

Below: Members of the Tom Gerun Orchestra, with Woody on clarinet, in San Francisco in 1932. *Rocky Mt. Photo Co.*

Above: Members of the Isham Jones Orchestra in 1936, with the leader seated at center and Woody kneeling at far right.

Below: By 1937, the Woody Herman Orchestra had grown to fourteen members. *Bill Burton*

Above: Woody with Charlotte and daughter, Ingrid.

Left: Early promotion photo for Woody Herman and His Orchestra. *James J. Kriegsmann*

Below: Woody and Ingrid, age three.

ove: Woody and Benny Goodman jamming in the 1940s.

pposite top: Tommy Dorsey (left) chatting with Benny Goodman and Woody in the
d-1940s.

ft: Benny Goodman (left) and Vaughn Monroe huddle with Woody at a Manhattan club in
e 1940s. *Jack Pyle*

Above: With Tennessee Williams in the 1940s. *Albert Freeman*

Below: The Andrews Sisters and actress Claire Trevor (second from left) with Woody in the early 1940s.

Joe DiMaggio greeting Woody at a ballpark.

Woody and Tony Martin at the Hollywood Palladium in the 1940s. *Gene Lester*

Above: Bing Crosby with Woody at the recording session for "Deep in the Heart of Texas" in 1942.

Below: Woody and Charlotte (second from right) taking a break with Spade Cooley, who led a Western swing band that was booked in 1947 by Woody's office. Woman at right is unidentified. *Floyd McCarty, Warner Bros.*

bove: Woody and unidentified man watching Igor Stravinsky at work during New York
hearsal of "Ebony Concerto" in 1946.

elow: Igor Stravinsky making a point to Chubby Jackson (left), Don Lamond (center), and Flip
hillips (right) during "Ebony Concerto" rehearsal in Manhattan in 1946. *Hauser and Tischler*

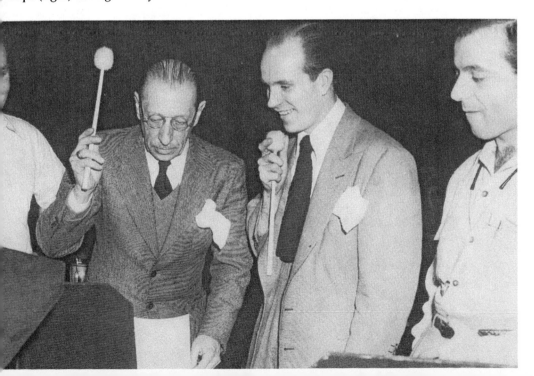

Above: Woody, who was an auto-racing fan, with Mel Torme (right) and unidentified driver at a California track in the late 1940s. *Don Mohr Studio*

Below: President Lyndon B. Johnson greeting Woody at the White House in 1965.

Woody with his old high school teacher and mentor, Sister Fabian, at a benefit in Milwaukee for the Sister Fabian Scholarship Fund.

Woody and Charlotte (far right) during the South America tour in 1958.

Performing in an Armed Forces Radio show during World War II.
Armed Forces Radio Service

Woody greeting Johnny Merce
with Artie Shaw (between them
George Simon, and Woody's
grandson, Tom Littlefield, at
right, in July 1973, opening nig
for Woody's band at the St. Reg
Roof in Manhattan. *New Jersey
Newsphotos*

Woody singing at the Vine Stre
club in Hollywood during a 198
engagement. *W. G. Harris*

Above: Benny Goodman and Lionel
Hampton helping Woody celebrate his
opening at the King Cole Room of the
St. Regis in 1986. *Richard Laird*

Right: Lawrence Berk, president and
founder of the Berklee College of
Music in Boston, presenting Woody
with an honorary degree as Doctor of
Music in May 1977. Woody, recovering
from an auto accident, attended the
ceremony in a wheelchair.

The Second Herd at the Century Room, Hotel Commodore, in Manhattan, on April 20, 1948.

wanted. Maybe we didn't have a porterhouse, but we had everything else.

Perhaps the most important new member of the band during the fifties was pianist Nat Pierce, whose playing and arranging became an enormous asset. But Pierce was much more than that. Just having his spirit and his presence around was a treasure.

Nat Pierce recalls:

I learned an awful lot of things from Woody—how to pace the night, what tunes to play in what spot. He wasn't a slave driver, a Simon Legree; he kind of let things evolve. Woody always made it comfortable, more like you were working with him rather than for him. The ship was tight but it was loose at the same time.

I first joined in the fall of 1951 and stayed until the spring of 1955. And I rejoined the big band from 1961 to 1966. I did a little writing during the first period, but Ralph Burns was doing most of it. He would send in two or three charts a week, or six a month. Most of my writing for the band began in the late 1950s and, during the 1960s, I became the chief writer.

Abe Turchen saved our ass many times during the 1950s. I remember we were on TV, "The Big Show of 1952," with people like the Mills Brothers and Dinah Washington, and then we would go cross-country for about thirty days. A lot of times we bombed out money-wise. Sometimes there wasn't enough to meet the payroll, and Abe would call some bookie in New York and ask, "Who's playing tonight?" It could be basketball or baseball, it didn't matter what sport. He would bet on these games, and somehow by the time the night was over, he had all this money in his hands.

There was a lot of scuffling going on. It wasn't easy. But it's never easy.

In the fall of 1953, a rich fellow from Chicago who was interested in early jazz financed a long tour of high schools and colleges in Illinois with a package that featured the band with

Sidney Bechet and Billy Eckstine. The following year, the band went to Europe for the first time. When we went to England in 1957, however, we were an Anglo-American band—half and half—because of British rules.

What helped us stay afloat was a three-month State Department tour of South America in 1958. Musically it was great. But we had to endure some white-knuckle trips on local airlines. We seemed to have close calls every other day. It reminded me of a wild trip the band had stateside with our own Air Force near the end of World War II.

We had a movie deal coming up on the West Coast, and the Air Force offered to pick up the band in Jackson, Michigan, and fly us to somewhere in New Mexico, then to California. There was a lot of ad-libbing in the services, and they were able to send us out on a big bomber.

When we arrived at the air base in New Mexico, the commanding officer who came to greet us was so drunk that everything he said was double-talk. So I immediately played a chorus of "Straighten Up and Fly Right." Then they put us on another plane for the trip to the coast. Our pilot tried to come down three times in the Los Angeles river. He thought it was a runway. Talk about the thrill of your pants.

Some of the planes we had to take on the South American trip in 1958 were old and decrepit. We cheered when we were booked on a DC-3. The pilots didn't have the same savvy we were used to on stateside flights—the Air Force incident notwithstanding.

Major Holley, the bass player on the South American tour, recalls:

Charlotte was along on a lot of the tour and she used to like to sit next to me. When we were on Panagra Airlines, which is no longer in existence, we went all through the Andes in Chile, and I mean through those mountains, to Peru and Ecuador. Panagra supplied good planes. We liked that. When we got into the warmer climes, flying on the aircraft that belonged to various other airlines, you could actually see the ground through holes in the bottom of the planes, where seats had been removed and the holes hadn't been filled. We were flying over hostile Indians, and desert and jungle in some of those aircraft. One time, we loaded up somewhere in central South America and the plane was too heavy. The pilot tried three times to take off. It was a regularly scheduled airline. I didn't realize it at the time, but we couldn't get enough altitude, and we came back and tried it again. It still didn't work. We almost crashed on that one.

Charlotte hadn't realized that we would be flying through the mountains, and she was paralyzed by it. This was before high-flying jets. When people think about Rio and all those wonderful places we went to, they forget how we got there.

In Bolivia, they have the highest airport in the world, and we couldn't breathe up there. They had oxygen on the stage for us.

At a couple of airports, they wouldn't let me take my bass inside the cabin. I didn't have much say about it; all the business was handled by Dick Turchen, Abe's nephew, along with Woody and Al Banner, the band boy.

In some places I found some of the same apparent racism that I've found in the States. Why would a soldier pick me out while we were all sitting in an airport terminal in Colombia and take his gun butt and hit me on my feet? My feet weren't blocking the aisle. He was trying to say something to me. When he found out I was with the rest of the group, he let me alone. Being the only black man in the group, he obviously thought that I didn't belong.

At a school concert in Peru, the students wouldn't let us inside, so the soldiers had to come to open the gates for us. The school had a thing about not allowing the bad students to attend the concert, and they were upset and surrounded the place. After we got inside to play, the soldiers left. When the concert was over, we couldn't get out until they brought the soldiers back.

The receptions for the band were great, lovely. We had big press all the time, and we played every kind of location, even in bull rings and outdoors, next to swimming pools for the elite. Once in Chile we played for an audience composed entirely of men. They got me to make a speech. I have just a small working knowledge of Spanish, and people were telling me what to say. It turned out I was calling these people all kinds of names, and they were breaking up because I didn't know what I was saying.

Some of the guys in the band resented me after a while because I always had a solo. With so little big band experience, I didn't think about how important it was for guys to have solos. They didn't get a lot of space, and I was featured every night, doing my little Slam Stewart act. I got a lot of press on that trip; they called me El Bajo. My solo was on "The Preacher," the piece by Horace Silver. It was a Nat Pierce arrangement.

In Venezuela, soldiers surrounded the plane and wouldn't let anybody off. Americans weren't very popular there at the time. [Then–Vice President Richard Nixon had had difficulty in Venezuela, as had Secretary of State John Foster Dulles.] We weren't concerned with politics. We just did our thing. It was a great, crazy experience. I'm glad I had a chance to go.

One day I went into a store in Brazil to buy some gifts, and a black guy followed me inside. He was Brazilian and he just wanted to meet me. The saleslady called the police because she thought we were going to rob the place. Later, the consulate held a party for us after our concert, and the same chick saleslady who had called the police was there. She tried to apologize, but I wasn't having any.

Woody was very humorous. Guys in South America try to get you coming and going with gold rings, jewelry, and things. Willie Thomas, the trumpeter, bought this ring that he was proud of. We were at a consulate or embassy party after a concert one night, and Woody said to him, "Let me see that ring." Woody looked at it a moment and then set it into one of the deviled eggs on the table and handed the egg to Willie.

In Jamaica, we checked into our hotel and they took Woody to his room. He opened the door and there was a lizard sitting on the wall. Woody just closed the door and split.

The trip, which began in July, ended about October. We did Central and South America and the Caribbean Islands. And I went through that whole tour without getting a scratch on my bass. But when I boarded an Eastern Airlines flight in New Orleans, they wouldn't let me bring it into the cabin. When I got it back in New York, the bass looked like a Christmas goose, neck hanging down and broken. They paid for it.

I first joined Woody's band the year before, after I came back from living in England for five years. Nat Pierce had a band in New York that I was playing some gigs with, but it was mainly a rehearsal band. Nat was the one who introduced me to everybody in Woody's band. They had been trying different bass players, and I guess I had the big tone that they needed.

We worked around the United States in 1957, traveling by bus mostly. I had sat in with the Second Herd a couple of times in the late forties, substituting for Oscar Pettiford, when Woody had Terry Gibbs, Shelly Manne, Mary Ann McCall, Ray Wetzel, and Tiny Kahn. The last place I ran into that band was at the Apollo Theater in Harlem. For some reason, Oscar Pettiford didn't make all the shows, and I was working there with Rose Murphy, so I filled in. I found that I got along very well with Woody.

When I later joined the band, the first thing we did was make a record at the old Everest studios with Tito Puente, "Tito Meets Woody." Then we went out and played up and down the country.

I spent Thanksgiving night that year at the Fort Bragg Army base, because they still had that crap going on with segregation down south. The only place I was safe to sleep at night was at the Army base. I also got into a brief thing with prejudice when we played a concert at the University of Georgia. They didn't have anyplace for me to stay, so I stayed with a black family.

At a hall in a little town in Kentucky, I walked in with the bass on my back, wearing the old clothes that I traveled on the bus with. The people there thought I was a roadie. After I got dressed in my uniform to play, I stayed on the bandstand behind the stage during the breaks, and the cats went and got me some food.

But there were no incidents. Woody was always cool about that. He wouldn't tolerate any foolishness.

I stayed with Woody a couple of years or so. After the State Department tour, the big band toured for a while, and then Woody started taking out small groups. He had Howard McGhee one time and we went with him to Washington, D.C. Then we went out to Vegas; Seldon Powell and Gus Johnson were with us.

I used to call Woody the sheriff, because he always had that whistle. Once he blew that whistle on you, forget it, you were out the door. I only heard him call it a couple of times on players or on situations. He also would pull off his coat and rumble with you if that's the way it was. But it was a lot of fun working with Woody. He was always on an even keel. His was the best band I was ever in. I had to end it after a couple of years because I didn't want to travel in cars anymore, like we were doing with the small groups.

16

THE

DEALER

I began the sixties with a five-piece nightclub act, featuring Bill Chase, an outstanding trumpet player who had been with my big band, and charts by Nat Pierce. Our act also spotlighted tap dancer Steve Condos and singer/pianist Norma Douglas. We played for a month at the Waldorf Astoria in Manhattan.

We played dance sets at the Waldorf, and the maître d' would come over in his tux and stiff collar and say, "You can't play that music in here. The people are dancing too much." He wasn't selling any drinks.

We also performed at Freedomland, which was a rinky-dink version of Disneyland up in the Bronx. A booker tried to sell us in Las Vegas, but we got no takers.

Nat Pierce recalls:

At Freedomland, they wanted a big band, and I got some guys from New York, including Gus Johnson, Charlie Mariano, and Joe Newman—all people who'd never played with Woody before. We did that once in a while on weekends, using the big band and the five-piece nightclub act. All of us, meanwhile, were basically out of a job, including Woody, and we made trips on other weekends to Virginia, West Virginia, and Ohio for work.

When I formed the big band again in 1961, it was more of the same struggle. Despite some successes, including a Grammy Award in 1963 for the *Encore* album on the Phillips label, we were a scuffling organization.

By that time, Abe Turchen had become our overall business manager; he was installed in our office at 200 West 57th Street in Manhattan. In fact, the office of another Woody was in that building—Woody Allen—and I'd run into him on the elevator and say, "Hi, I'm the old one." He and I had to play clarinets together once on "The Tonight Show" and it was a horrible experience.

Abe had good business sense and lots of friends in the music business. He could convince people that we were saleable. Abe knew how to get things done. When he had started working with me as road manager in 1945, for example, he managed to overcome one of our biggest problems—transportation. Abe always found a way to keep us moving despite gasoline rationing.

I gave him control of everything because I felt he was qualified, despite his penchant for gambling.

Abe was quite a guy. He was about five-foot-nine, and weighed about 200, which was his weight when he was a sergeant in the Marine Corps. Out of shape, he was about 250. He was a man about town who loved the show business world and had a particular fondness for certain comics, such as Fat Jack E. Leonard. He knew that I knew all of them, and that became his entry into hanging out with them.

At the office, he was wheeling and dealing alone. Well, almost alone. He had a habit of inviting everybody in who needed a job. That's how he would show kindness, by giving them office space. The whole outer office was usually loaded with bookmakers, money lenders, and others he was doing business with.

Nat Pierce recalls:

When I was road manager in the sixties, we had a contract for a while at Harrah's in Reno and Lake Tahoe, six weeks each. Basically it was just cowboys and Indians there, but there was gambling.

Abe would get fifty percent of our money up front, so I was operating with the fifty percent we collected at the engagements, and I would put a little money in a bank account we established in Reno. One night, I was totally out and playing craps, just throwing hundred dollar bills on the field. I think I lost about four or five thousand that night. I was sick, and I called Abe in New York. All he could do was laugh. Even Woody laughed.

"You've got to be kidding," Woody said.

I wrote plenty of arrangements for years to make up for it.

A few times Abe came out and played at the blackjack table. When I lost some of the band's money, I said to him, "I need twenty-five hundred." He said, "Don't worry about it. You stand here and I'll call you over." He called me over and gave me about seven hundred. Then he said, "How much more you need?" I told him, and later he called me back and gave me more. "You got enough now?" Yeah.

They finally barred him he was winning so much.

In Los Angeles, we played a place called Basin Street West, where we made the record that won the Grammy. Our engagement was an unqualified success. We came back there six or eight months later, and business was still pretty good. But I couldn't get any money. There were these strange people coming in and out of the club every evening, some of them carrying paper bags. They were apparently siphoning off the money. When I went to get the pay, there wasn't any. Woody was up in his house, and I called him and said, "What should we do?"

We bounced a few checks for gasoline money, so we could get to the next gig in Tahoe. When I didn't have money to get us out of Tahoe, everybody came up with a little cash to put gasoline in the bus.

Later on, Abe was taking all the money and I wasn't able to operate the band. I called him from a phone booth in the desert in Texas, and told him that if the money wasn't where we were going, we weren't going to be able to operate. Sometimes the money was there.

Besides being the business manager, Abe tried to get us jobs because, during the fifties, Joe Glazer and, later, Willard Alexander weren't getting us enough bookings.

Abe also had other business things going. Early on, he had bought land on an island off San Diego. He built three luxury houses there and lived in one of them himself. But that wasn't fast-enough action for him. He had many different things that he became involved in for short periods. We set up a personal management office in New York once, in which I tried to work with him to help develop people. But he became bored with that, too. Not enough action.

Gene Lees recalls:

While I was editor of down beat, *from 1959 to the fall of 1961, Wood came through Chicago with the only sloppy band I ever heard him have. The band was ragged and he was in a profound depression. I got drunk with him.*

It was the first time I had formally met him. When I was fifteen, I tried to get his autograph in Toronto. I tried to strike up a conversation with him, which can be very annoying to a person in a position of public celebrity. He sloughed me off, and I was very hurt. I carried a small resentment for years over it.

Now here I was at down beat *in Chicago, and I had an interview with him, and we ended up getting plastered. I began to sense a different person than the impression that I'd had. Woody could be abrasive, never cruel. But he had a tough streak in him along with the sweetness. He was road-hardened.*

Sometime after that, I left down beat *and came to New York.*

Woody had a septet at that time with Zoot Sims, Nat Adderley, Jake Hanna, and Nat Pierce. They were playing upstairs at the Metropole, and I went there with Marian McPartland. We sat with him and the guys, and he made a remark that stuck in my mind like glue. He said, "I never was much of a clarinet player." And I absolutely fell in love with the man in that split second. It's that vivid in my mind.

I was having a difficult time getting established in New York— living at the West Side Y and getting locked out of my room regularly, when I couldn't pay my rent. It was late in 1961. Woody and Abe Turchen said to me essentially: "You shouldn't be living like this, this hand-to-mouth existence. Wood suggested that I come to work for them.

"Doing what?" I asked.

"Who cares," Wood said. "Doing the publicity."

So I went to work for him doing publicity. By this time, he had organized the band that recorded for Phillips, the band with Bill Chase, the band that played standing up at the Metropole. It was one of the great bands he had, rich in soloists like Bill Chase and Sal Nistico. It was wonderfully disciplined.

He built that band but I built its image. I started out writing pieces for publications in which it was easy to plant stories. I did the second-line publications first, then I went after the biggies. It worked. It wasn't a hard sell. It might have happened without me, but I think Wood always felt that what I did that year was very important.

We all loved Abe Turchen. He was a pessimistic realist. He reminded me of Jack E. Leonard. He talked like Jack; he was very friendly, very overweight, homely, diabetic, and he chewed his fingernails. He used to try to tell Jewish jokes with a New York accent, and he couldn't do it. He was from the Midwest. The jokes were awful, and Abe was inadvertently funny.

He was a chronic gambler. He used to sit in that office, with piles of papers on his desk, picking up the phone, watching television, playing solitaire, and booking the band all at the same time.

Lou Singer, the songwriter, shared the office in the other room of the suite. Abe had his office in the front of the building, and he'd be placing bets on the phone. Once I had to take his car and go out to Brooklyn and collect an envelope of money for him. I went to Lundy's in Sheepshead Bay and I sat there at the bar waiting, as instructed, and this guy comes up to me and hands me an envelope and says, "Count it." I took it back to Abe.

Sometimes the envelopes of cash went out, too. I assumed that it was Abe's money, and maybe it was.

Woody called the office one day and asked me to get so-and-so's address from the files. I laughed. "The files? What files?"

That was the sloppiest operation in history. But I understood Woody's feeling about the man. Abe would find him supermarket openings to play—the weirdest gigs in the weirdest places—and he kept that band working; he kept those salaries flowing.

Abe would sit back in his chair with his damn TV set going all day long. His cards and his phones and his betting were going on in a kind of soup of activity. I didn't pay any attention to it. All I knew was that the band worked. I was busy trying to get stories done on the band.

Sometime in 1963, I wrote lyrics for Bill Evans' "Waltz for Debbie," at Bill's request. A woman in Sweden named Monica Zetterling recorded it. I was sent a copy of the record and I gave it to Mort Fega, the disc jockey, and Mort started playing it on the air, mentioning who had written the lyric. Woody happened to hear it on the radio while riding in from the airport in a taxi.

He walked into the office and said to me, "Why didn't you tell me you could write lyrics like that?"

"You didn't ask me," I said.

He called Howie Richmond and within forty-eight hours I was signed to a nice sustaining contract, which is how I came to write all the things with Charles Aznavour, who was doing a lot of stuff for Howie. That gave me enough money to live on. Then a few things happened for me in succession: A novel of mine was published, Tony Bennett recorded two or three of my lyrics, including "Quiet Nights." I was getting really busy, doing a lot of freelancing. And Woody didn't need me anymore. The publicity was beginning to generate itself.

He came in off the road to work the Metropole in 1963, after I had been with him a year or so. I went to lunch with him, and I explained that I was having a problem.

"What's the problem?" he asked.

I said, "Essentially, you don't need me anymore. And I, on the other side of the coin, am up to my eyes in work."

He said, "What's the problem? What are you trying to tell me?"

"I don't have time to do it anymore," I said.

"I still don't understand what the problem is."

"I really hate to leave you and the band."

"If that's all there is to it," he said, "I'll make it simple for you. You're fired. Now let's have lunch."

He went around for years afterward introducing me as the only man he ever fired.

I didn't think Abe Turchen's yen for gambling would get in the way. But there were plenty of clues, if I had been more attentive. While I was playing somewhere in Europe in the late fifties, for example, Abe telephoned to say we had to sell my music publishing company, Charlin, because he needed more financing for what we were doing.

"Forget it," I told him. "Charlin is my legacy to Charlotte and Ingrid."

But Abe had power of attorney as business manager, and he sold it out from under me.

By the mid-sixties, I had fallen into a financial stranglehold from which I would never recover.

17
THE IRS
DEBACLE

The first I learned of how much trouble I was in was when the Internal Revenue Service sent me a letter ordering me to appear in person. Until then, the IRS had been corresponding with my office, and Abe Turchen never gave me a clue about it.

I arrived at the tax office with Abe and learned that, not only had my personal income taxes been unpaid for 1964 through 1966, so had the withholding taxes on the musicians' salaries. The punishment was a tax bill of about $750,000, with interest and penalties over the years bringing the figure to $1.6 million.

I sat there, stunned.

I never believed their figures. All the years in which we had big grosses—not big profits—we paid taxes to the hilt.

Here I was down and out in the sixties, and the IRS was basing its estimate of my debt on years when our revenues had been high.

Charlotte was appalled at how stupid we had been in our judgment of Abe. But I felt as responsible as Abe for the mess.

Gene Lees observes:

Woody was the oddest mixture of shrewd perception and pure naïveté. He could be almost cunningly observant of people. Yet I believe he was utterly unaware of what Abe had done. What Woody was guilty of was not paying attention. That was the nature of the problem.

I never went into a state of shock over it. I was depressed for a moment or two, but I knew that I had to get back to the business of music in order to take care of it as best I could. We worked out an arrangement to pay the government $1,000 a week through whomever was booking us. But we couldn't always afford it; we had to renegotiate.

My lawyers worked hard to help get me off the hook somehow. I saw what the government had done to Joe Louis, forcing him to wind up as a handshaking shill for a Las Vegas hotel. I would have preferred going to jail than to finish like that. But I never considered imprisonment as a threat. I always figured the IRS would have less to gain with me behind bars.

For some unearthly reason, I kept Abe on the job. But by August 1968, I couldn't take any more.

Bill Byrne, who joined the trumpet section of the band in 1965, recalls:

Nat Pierce and Bill Chase were the road managers, splitting the duties, when I arrived. Abe Turchen got me to do it in 1967, when we were playing the Riverboat in the Empire State Building for a month. I left for a while, and Woody, meanwhile, got rid of Abe.

Every week a bus company would come up to the band with a subpoena, because Abe hadn't paid. And they would try to take the band's music library. Woody just got fed up with it.

Abe died in San Diego some years ago. All that time Woody didn't say anything publicly about Abe. Woody liked characters, and Abe was a Damon Runyon classic.

When I fired Abe Turchen, I took on Hermie Dressel as business manager. He was the only guy who would accept it. I had talked to others who could handle the job. Norman Granz, for example, said, "Thanks, I think it's a great honor. But no thanks."

Willard Alexander's office was booking the band, but he had no faith in us. He had his favorites, such as Count Basie and the Glenn Miller ghost band.

Funny thing was that in 1966, one of the tax years in contention, we made another State Department tour, this one to Algeria, Morocco, the Congo, Uganda, Tanzania, Yugoslavia, and Romania. Among the guys in that band were Ronnie Zito on drums, Marvin Stamm and Bill Chase on trumpets, Carl Fontana on trombone, and Nat Pierce on piano.

Nat Pierce recalls:

On the way, we landed in Madrid for an overnight stay, and they took all the music and Woody's alto sax, put them in a big cage and padlocked it. We went into town and had a nice dinner. At the airport the next morning, the cage was empty.

"What happened?" we asked. They said they put it on the plane. But when we got to Dar es Salaam, there was no music and no alto sax. We were able to borrow an alto down there, but Woody couldn't even get a noise out of it. We got the music back a few days later, but the alto didn't come back for a couple of years.

We were playing a reception for the second vice president of Tanzania, and I had to write out the Tanzanian national anthem for the band. I thought I'd doctor it up a little and put some flashy things in for Bill Chase to play. We were rehearsing it in the room in which we were to play while workers were up on step ladders decorating the place with crepe paper and banners. When we started to play it and Bill started playing the flashy stuff, the workers started coming down off the ladders and coming toward the band. I said, "Uh-oh, we'd better leave out that Bill Chase part."

The band sounded the worst during that gig, because we had no music and there were some new guys in the band. Also, Woody couldn't play the same things on clarinet that he could play on alto.

Bill Byrne recalls:

Beginning in 1966, we also started making annual European tours, mostly to England, for about ten straight years. When we first started going over there, we played double concerts, with full houses most of the time—one at six and one at nine. As years went along, it dwindled to one concert a night, which was easier on us.

In 1970 we went to Japan for George Wein. We also hit Hong Kong, Singapore, and Bangkok. Great receptions. In 1966, we did a European and English tour, and then to Africa.

We used to have a booker in Sweden named Boo Johnson, and he took us to Poland for about five years in a row during the mid- and late seventies. Woody was treated like royalty because his mother was born there. We also played Finland, Norway, Sweden, Denmark, East Germany, for Boo.

Among other notable foreign trips was one to South America in 1980, and a couple of tours of Europe and Australia in 1985 with the big band and with small groups—one that included Harry (Sweets) Edison, Buddy Tate, Al Cohn, Jake Hanna, John Bunch, and a bass player from Toronto, and another with Nat Pierce replacing John, and without Tate.

I was tired, but I kept plugging away because I loved the music, I had an overwhelming need to make a living, and the government wouldn't have looked kindly on my retirement.

18
A NEW PUSH

I had a speech I gave to all kids in junior high schools, high schools, and sometimes in colleges. I told them to be as independent and together about their music as they possibly could be. And to find some other way to earn a living, because they would have a better life. I would suggest possibly a career in electronics or computers, so they could get into the swim of what's happening today. I told them to use their music as something to help keep their minds and their hearts straight.

Weird. Here I was making an appeal to youngsters and ignoring the music that moved them. The emergence of rock and roll was making it tougher to get bookings, but I wasn't going to be bulldozed by it. The secret, I figured, was to explore its most inventive offerings and make them swing.

And I got some timely help from a young pianist.

Alan Broadbent recalls:

I was twenty-one when I left the Berklee School of Music in Boston and joined Woody's band in 1969. Woody was just starting to get guys from schools like North Texas State and Berklee. Bill Byrne was there and Frank Tiberi was there. Sal Nistico rejoined the band a couple of times.

It wasn't really that glamorous when I first joined the band. All we were doing were Army bases and Elks clubs. We weren't yet doing college things. It was kind of a slump period.

But Woody was doing some contemporary things like "Mac-Arthur Park" and "Light My Fire." I had to find a way to introduce myself to Woody as a writer. The hot group of the time was Blood, Sweat and Tears, and they did a tune called "Smiling Phases," which featured jazz soloing. I did a chart on it and we rehearsed it without Woody. We had a prom coming up. Woody wanted to hear it at the prom, and the kids went wild. We also did "Proud Mary," a Creedence Clearwater Revival piece.

Then I figured I'd do another tune, a ballad, and we tried it again without Woody at a rehearsal. I tried to use all my Berklee training and my Gil Evans voicings, and mutes and woodwinds. Well, it just didn't work, acoustically or any way when we played it on the bandstand. It started falling apart. The band sort of petered out at the end. Woody looked at me as if to say, "Is that it?" And I said, "Yeah." That was a major lesson for me.

After that, we had a big Las Vegas gig, which gave me a regular place to stay, because I lived on the bus.

Woody was kind of intrigued by "Smiling Phases" and all this Blood, Sweat and Tears stuff. He said, "Why don't you do something with 'Blues in the Night?' " I spent the next month or so thinking about it, writing out little sketches and things. I threw in everything I could think of, including the bridge. I put in baroque things; I always had this flair for the grandiose; I knew the ending was going to be big. When I had pieced it together, and we rehearsed it, Woody just loved it. The best recording of it was when he did it in 1976 at Carnegie Hall for the Fortieth Anniversary concert.

Then we did an album with Mike Bloomfield, a blues guitar player, for Fantasy records.

I did about fifteen or sixteen charts altogether for the band. The major charts Woody left as is. There were a few things he suggested. But I think there were a couple of rock charts in which he put different motifs in different places. He knew exactly what it was that would make a chart sound good.

In 1970, we made a tour of the Far East and we played a high-falutin businessmen's club in Tokyo. There was another band performing on the other stage, and we alternated sets. We had this thing on the ending of "MacArthur Park," a big show biz ending with the five trumpet players going into different corners of the room, and there would be this big improvisation. Buddy Powers, the second trumpet player, went out with the others to the corners for this big climax, and suddenly they started improvising. Buddy was standing halfway back in the room near some tables. This Japanese businessman was so affronted by the trumpet playing near him that he took his drink and threw it in Buddy's face.

One of the guys on the bandstand watched it happen and said, "Did you see that?" Buddy came back to the bandstand all flabbergasted and wet. Woody went over to Buddy, while we were still playing the ending, and asked him what happened. Then he took his clarinet, removed the cap from the mouthpiece, and slowly walked out into the audience, smiling at everybody. He came up to the table of the guy who threw the drink and squawked and squeaked his clarinet directly at him. We were in hysterics. The gigantic ending had to last an extra few minutes while Woody did his thing at that table.

Woody was very protective of us. I guess it was a real paternal thing, which is why he's always been called the Road Father.

I was young and I wasn't taking care of myself too well. By the end of the third year, I just didn't want to be part of the road anymore. Woody understood that. I gave him a lot of notice. But it was always hard for him, I think, to let that go. He saw it so many times with guys he really felt for. I could sense that he was hurt, letting a son go. It was the same way he felt about Sal Nistico.

It was a very special thing. He always knew when you were up, when you were creating. He could always make that intense moment yours. If you were improvising, having a good time, he never stomped on you.

But I don't have very fond memories of being on the road. Bill Byrne was the saviour for us all, Woody included. All the shit would just roll off his back. He'd get pissed off, but it was such an honest pissed off, and two minutes later it would be gone and he'd be so apologetic. Somehow he managed to keep everybody going.

I continued to write for Woody for two years after I left the band. My favorite charts were "Bebop and Roses" and "Far In." And a few of the ballads, one that I did for [trumpet player] Tom Harrell, "A Time for Love."

Gene Lees recalls:

Woody had an astonishing capacity to spot talent before it was particularly obvious to anybody else. Two fine examples were Kenny Ascher and Alan Broadbent. Woody asked me to work with both of them. Ascher, who was arranging and playing piano in the band in the sixties, and I wrote one or two songs together, but they didn't go anywhere. With Alan, I had listened to some of his charts and playing and I couldn't see it for sour apples. But Woody kept telling me how gifted this guy was, that this was a guy I should write with.

Today I consider Alan Broadbent one of the greatest pianists in jazz and a marvelous composer. Woody saw that talent when it was in a very germlike stage.

He made careers; he had a lot to do with mine. But the list of careers that he either made or advanced is staggering.

We gathered new strength in 1973 from the *Giant Steps* album on Fantasy, which earned us a Grammy. Most of the arrangements were made by trumpet player Bill Stapleton, including the title cut, composed by John Coltrane. It also contained Alan Broadbent's "Bebop and Roses" and an arrangement of "La Fiesta" by Tony Klatka.

When Broadbent left the band, our drummer, Joe La-Barbera, recommended Harold Danko to replace him.

Harold Danko recalls:

I joined the band in April 1972, and stayed through October. I was in the Army when I got the call from Bill Byrne. I was discharged on April 3, and I joined the band April 6. I had had no idea what I was going to do after I got out of the Army. All of a sudden I had a great gig.

Al Johnson was on bass, Al Porcino was on lead trumpet, Bobby Burgess was lead trombone, Frank Tiberi on sax. I think everyone who went through the band learned a lot from Frank.

I had good coaching from drummer Joe LaBarbera for getting on with Woody. He briefed me and gave me tapes. He said, "Don't bother saying hello to Woody. Just go out and do the gig." And he hipped me to a couple of Woody's tests for incoming pianists. Joe said, "Do you know Duke's intro to 'Satin Doll' and 'A-Train'?" I said yes. He said, "Well, Woody's liable to call them, and if you play just a normal intro, he knows you don't know the shit."

Sure enough, on the first gig I didn't bother saying hello to Woody. He came on the bandstand and said to me, " 'Satin Doll,' intro." So I played it.

Shortly after I joined, we went into the studio to record "The Raven Speaks." It was my first record date, and I was thrilled. Thinking aloud, I felt that this was a piece of history, recording with Woody Herman. The session was in New York City. Some of the stuff we were reading for the first time. One of the pieces we did was "Bill's Blues," a blues in A-flat, written by Bill Stapleton. He was a great trumpet player and writer in the band. I had two choruses on it up front. So of course I tried to tell my whole life's story in these two choruses of A-flat blues, playing whatever I felt I knew. The band came in not quite right. Take one didn't quite work. I don't know if I played a horrible solo. Maybe I did.

We did another take, and I think I tried even harder at that point. I felt, Jeezus, I gotta play my ass off. Again the band didn't come in quite right. And Woody came up to me and said, "Harold, it's only an intro."

The band was another powerhouse. When Harold Danko left, we formed a new rhythm section with Andy LaVerne on piano, Ed Soph on drums, Wayne Darling on bass, Joe Beck on guitar. We also had some crackling horn soloists—Stapleton on trumpet, Jim Pugh on trombone, and Greg Herbert on tenor sax.

The following year, we collected another Grammy, this one for *Thundering Herd* on the Fantasy label.

Considering the climate for big bands, even one that was experimenting with electronic piano and some jazz-rock charts, we were getting good receptions, particularly at colleges, where we had begun to do combination concerts-clinics.

The University of Houston honored me by establishing the Woody Herman Music Archives at its School of Music. Initially, I gave them record albums, original scores of "The Woodchopper's Ball" and other hits, along with some instruments. The man who made the biggest contribution to the archives, however, was my longtime friend Jack Siefert, who had collected and chronicled material on me and the bands since we first met in 1937.

Jack Siefert recalls:

I took off the entire summer of 1974 to put together the Woody Herman archives. I did it in chronological order—every single tune, every version, cross-indexed. My wife, Mary, did the typing and my kids did all the indexing.

I took thirty-three reels of tape to Houston; and I made a bound volume of the index. When I got to Houston, I went to Neiman-Marcus with these suitcases full of tapes and asked to have them gift-wrapped. The store clerk asked, "Were they bought here?" I said no. And he said, "Well, that's against our policy."

"Mr. Herman is donating this to the University of Houston," I said. "I'm just a courier."

"Oh," he said, "in that case . . ." and he wrapped up the book and the suitcases in gold. He charged me the minimum of about two dollars.

There was a big ceremony at the University of Houston. Woody was so proud. I felt so good. He hadn't expected it to be that amount of work. But I said, "Woody, this is your life."

He was the kind of friend for whom there was nothing I wouldn't do. When he would go to Europe, say for six weeks, he would park his Corvette at our house near Philadelphia, rent a car for the drive to the New York airport, and dump it. Meanwhile, we'd have his car serviced. When he would return, and he'd have a day or two off, he used to go to the school to pick up our kids. The kids just loved him. They'd get in his Corvette, sometimes with their friend who was crazy about the car, and he would drive them home. That's the real Woody Herman.

He was at our house one night during the sixties, and tried to telephone his father, who was in a nursing home. He called and called, and finally a nurse answered and said, "I'm sorry, but we can't rouse your father. He doesn't know who you are."

Woody hung up and he had tears in his eyes. "Dad didn't know who I was," he said. In an effort to comfort him, I said, "That's a shame, you went to all that trouble." Woody put his arm around me and said, "Jack, the important thing is that I knew who he was." He had a keen understanding of what was important.

And nobody realizes what a lady Charlotte was.

Mary Siefert recalls:

One of the many times Charlotte came to the house was when Woody was being honored at the White House by Lyndon Johnson. She stayed here to get her wardrobe ready while Woody was doing one-nighters in the area. It happened to be around Christmas time. Jack and I had been invited to several parties.

I said to Charlotte, "I have to find another something to wear."

She said, "Well, what would you like to wear?"

It was the time when long skirts were beginning to come back in fashion. I said, "I would like a nice long skirt, a nice red velvet skirt."

She suggested we go to a store, because she wanted to buy some material. She made me this gorgeous red velvet skirt. She was marvelous with her hands.

And Woody was probably the Duncan Hines of the music business. He could tell you the best restaurant in any big city or small town, and invariably he was right. He remembered where they were and exactly what he ate in every one of them.

Jack Siefert adds:

When I was traveling for my company, I used to say to Woody, "Hey, I'm going to Cincinnati."

"Three places," he'd reply. "This one's the best." Same thing whether I was going to Chicago or to Denver. He knew every restaurant.

Sometimes I would be amazed to see someone come up to him at an engagement and ask for a Glenn Miller tune. Woody never did that even when he was recording cover tunes. If he was in the right mood, he'd lean over and say, "I'll tell you what, next time I see Glenn Miller I'll tell him you requested that."

He was sick as a dog one day at our house and he had to go play at a place about a hundred miles away. We had a station wagon with a four-inch mattress in the back, and Mary added a pillow. I drove down there, with Woody lying in the back. We had some medicine for him. He made the performance, and a lady came up to him and said, "You know, I remember you from Old Orchard, Maine, back in 1940, and you don't look the same." He looked at her, and he said, "You know, I remember you from Old Orchard, Maine, too . . ."

Before he could say anything else, she turned to her husband and said, "He remembers me?"

Then Woody turned to me and said, "I guess I'm losing my touch. I was gonna say I recognized the dress."

Right after that he went to Annapolis to play a dance. He was really sick. After the first set, he started sweating, and he announced, "Is there a doctor in the house?" There was a doctor—a man who coincidentally had played in the band briefly in the forties. So he took Woody backstage to lie down. Woody said to me, "I want them to know that I'm not on drugs, that I'm sick. I want the doctor to tell them; he's one of theirs."

The doctor came back and said, "You have a 102 temperature. You have the flu." The doctor announced to the crowd: "Ladies and gentlemen, I have known Woody for years. In the true show business tradition he came out here tonight. But he has no business being here with the flu. He should be in bed."

The whole place roared. We flew him to New York, and he was out for about a week.

In the house that I had, we set aside a suite of rooms for him. I had a room downstairs with a piano and bar and a jazz room with all the stuff. We called it Wood's Hole. Woody considered our home his eastern pit stop.

I'm a working engineer, so my hours were different than his. When he would visit, I'd try to keep up. But by the fourth night in a row, I'd just fall down. We were coming home at one-thirty in the morning, Mary would make something to eat, and we'd sit and talk until four. And I got up at five-thirty. He would sleep until eleven-thirty or noon, and have long conversations during the day with Mary. She said it was like talking to your brother. Woody would talk about his mother, about Charlotte, and about Ingrid. He was just a warm human being, the warmest I ever met. He had the right sense of values.

We stopped numbering the Herds after the third one, but we were still thundering across the country nicely in the seventies, me by car, the band by bus and plane—until fatigue on one bright summer afternoon in 1977 almost ended it all.

LOSS

19

OF FREEDOM

Driving across the country, from tank town to city to tank town, gave me the feeling of independence I had enjoyed since I first left Milwaukee in my Whippet to join Tom Gerun's band in Chicago.

I made practically all the jumps by car. If the band had to travel 7,000 miles, I drove 7,000 miles, sometimes alone, sometimes with Charlotte. In the late fifties and sixties, with Bill Chase, who was an avid motor fan.

But the law of averages caught up with me in March of 1977. I was alone in a rented car—my Corvette was being worked on somewhere—and on my way to Kansas State University from somewhere in central Kansas. I had left central Kansas around ten in the morning and it wasn't long before

I realized I was sleepy. It was cumulative tiredness, fatigue. I stopped two or three times to walk around the car.

It was a lovely summer day, about two in the afternoon. I was driving along a regular two-lane highway near Fort Reilly, which is an old Army camp. Maybe fifty or a hundred yards from the main gate of the camp, I fell asleep. I crashed head-on into another car.

No one was hurt seriously in the other car, thank God. But the wreck practically demolished my leg. They took me to St. Mary's Hospital in Manhattan, Kansas, where they had to put steel pins in my leg up to my hip. I stayed there about four weeks and went home for therapy.

The band continued to tour with Frank Tiberi at the helm, and Buddy DeFranco fronted the band on a few dates.

On May 14, 1977, just a couple of days before my sixty-fourth birthday, I was still in a wheelchair when I took a flight to the Berklee College of Music in Boston to receive an honorary degree as Doctor of Music.

By the first week in June, I was back in front of the band. My driving days were over. I missed the freedom of making my own schedules. But in the long run, it was less tiring to take buses and planes or have someone drive me in a car from location to location.

I had recovered pretty well, but Charlotte was in the midst of her own major health crisis.

She had always been a very healthy woman. But she began to suffer from cancer in the early seventies. It started as breast cancer and then went through her body. She was operated on several times, but she was able to handle the situation well, between her spirit and the chemotherapy.

Gene Lees recalls:

Charlotte was an extremely beautiful woman, with flaming red hair, a crepe paper skin and gorgeous bone structure. The underlying structure of the face was so exquisite that even when her face became lined she remained beautiful.

She achieved a remarkable balance in her behavior toward the band. She had a sixth sense about how friendly to be. She was warm to the guys, never forbidding, never inaccessible. But she did not encourage people to get too close. She was very supportive of the musicians. She was diplomatic and knew exactly how to handle her situation with the band members.

I knew, of course, how bad she was. I had talked to her doctors and to my own, Dr. Stanley Levy in Detroit. He was losing his wife to cancer at about the same time. We had a lot in common. I knew Stan for about twenty-five years. I met him when I had an emergency while playing in Detroit. It was a blockage in my esophagus. I liked the way he handled my situation. He had put me in a hospital immediately and found the problem. After that, anytime I had a problem of any sort I would consult with him. He would advise me about surgeons or medication, or whatever I needed. He became more like a brother than a doctor.

Jack Siefert recalls:

Stanley Levy was one of the finest men I ever met in my life. He took care of Woody for twenty years. Wherever Woody was, he'd call Dr. Levy and Dr. Levy would call him back in twenty minutes.

He loved Woody. Dr. Levy made three-thousand-mile house calls. When I was operated on for a hernia, Woody was staying at our house. I came home, took some of the medication the doctor had given me, and I passed right out. I fell in the tub and cracked my ribs. Woody came in and said, "Let me get ahold of Dr. Levy."

He got through to him faster than I could have gotten a doctor in Philadelphia. Dr. Levy called back and said, "Let me talk to Jack." He told me, "Get off that medication." Here was Dr. Levy on the phone telling me what to do through Woody.

In 1976, we decided to arrange to celebrate my fortieth anniversary as a bandleader. We were trying for a date at Avery Fisher Hall in Manhattan when a cancellation at Carnegie Hall, for November 20, fit right into our plans. We managed to attract an all-star package of alumni. Flip Phillips, Chubby Jackson, Sam Marowitz, and Don Lamond came up from Florida. Nat Pierce and Jimmy Rowles shared piano duties with Ralph Burns, who took time out from a road tour for the reunion.

For the "Four Brothers," we had Stan Getz, Zoot Sims, Al Cohn, and Jimmy Giuffre. Jake Hanna, who had been a driving force in the band in the early sixties, played drums.

Pete and Conte Candoli added sparkle, along with Billy Bauer and Gary Anderson, who had written our arrangement of "Fanfare for the Common Man." Trombonist Jim Pugh, who played in the band in the early seventies, delivered a warm reading of "Everywhere," which Bill Harris had composed. Phil Wilson took the trombone choruses on "Bijou," which Ralph Burns had written for Harris. And Mary Ann McCall sang "Wrap Your Troubles in Dreams."

The concert was a smash, and was recorded by RCA. I was starting my fifth decade as a coach—a title I've always preferred over bandleader—on a high note.

20
NEW ORLEANS
EXPERIMENT

Among the unusual honors I've received occurred when the Zulu Society named me King of the Zulus for the New Orleans Mardi Gras parade in February 1980. Louis Armstrong was accorded the same tribute in 1949, but I was the first white person to be so named.

Afterward, Tom Gaskill of the Hyatt Regency Hotel in New Orleans came to see me. He loved our band, and he had approached a couple of outside people about building a room adjoining the hotel, and installing the band in it. I think that jealousy was among the reasons for wanting to do it. Pete Fountain's band was having great success attracting people to the Hilton.

It sounded like a dream idea to me, even a turning point

for helping big bands to survive. If we were able to repeat the kind of success Pete Fountain was having, hotel people around the country might say, "Hey, what's this?" What a way to cap off my later years.

Best of all, it would give us a home base from which to operate and help us reduce the constant traveling. That, in turn, would cut the normal, steady turnover of young musicians. And the bonus was having the time and place to rehearse. From that base thirty-six weeks a year we could arrange tours for the other months and have our pick of the best engagements. The reason for that is that when you're not available most of the time, the demand and the price go up.

The Hyatt Regency had a 9,000-foot shell that had been left unfinished next to the hotel, on the mall level of Poydras Plaza. The room, when it was completed, could hold 500 people, with theater-style seating. We opened Woody Herman's late in 1981.

A few problems accompanied us. Many of the fixtures and lights weren't yet in place, and the hotel had no budget for advertising; the funds had been used to build the room. If there had been sufficient publicity, everything might have been great. Instead, Woody Herman's was the best kept secret in New Orleans. We were performing six nights a week and I would run into locals on the street who asked me, "What are you doing in New Orleans?"

We stayed there a few months before going off on tour for a while. When we returned, we found the room the way we had left it—unfinished. The idea of having entertainment there during our absence, to solidify the place, went by the boards.

The backers never came up with the money they had promised, so we were operating at a loss from the beginning. And I wasn't able to depend on people I needed, such as Hermie Dressel, who was our business manager then.

It was a great disappointment, and not the only one. The bottom dropped out of what looked like a great deal to do three television shows with lots of guest stars. We shot it all in New Orleans, and it looked wonderful. Those shows are lying in a can somewhere in Florida. The whole thing was in litigation. Nobody got paid. I doubt if the shows will ever be shown, because of the money involved.

By the spring of 1982, the dream in New Orleans was failing. More important, Charlotte's condition had worsened. She had apparently given up. She stopped taking the chemotherapy, and she didn't want to go to the bedroom on the bottom level of the house any longer. She decided to spend her days and nights on a soft leather lounge on the second level, off the living room.

I was on the phone with her every day. Not a lot of people, outside of our personal friends, knew how sick she was. She tried to cover it; she wasn't the kind of person who would have wanted anyone to know that she was ill.

I had to go to her.

Jack Siefert recalls:

He told the guys in the band that he was going home and that the club was going dark. They understood.

As he was leaving from the airport the next day, some callous reporter approached him.

"Mr. Herman," he said, "I understand the club has gone dark and you're going home. What's the greatest record you ever made?"

Woody replied, "I've been married and in love with the same woman for forty-six years. Can you match that record?"

I went to see her at the hospital in Los Angeles and stayed at her bedside. One afternoon when Ingrid and I were visiting her, I was sitting on the edge of her bed, holding her hand, and I saw that she was failing. I started to sob. She summoned up what strength she had left, reached up, and punched me on the arm.

"Straighten up, Wood," she said. "We've been through tougher times than this."

I was with her in the hospital room when she died two weeks later.

A week later, I was back at work. It was the only therapy I knew, and I was sure the government wouldn't look kindly on a long hiatus.

Staying in one place too long isn't good for a man with a band. Being on the road gave me a certain kind of freedom to concentrate on the music and to play what I wanted. If you stay in one place too long, pretty soon you begin to play the music that someone else wants you to play. And you become nostalgic.

Nostalgia never appealed to me, spiritually or musically. In terms of the latter, there naturally were certain tunes closely associated with the band. That's often what people came out to hear, to stir their own memories. By the same token, I never felt the band's future was tied to delving into the past.

If I had to be confined to what I did when I was a young man, if I felt there weren't any more challenges besides doing that over and over again and polishing it a little more, I would have thrown in the towel. I couldn't have continued, because I was not built for the vaudeville era. I started that way, but I couldn't live by that kind of rule book.

Young players helped us to keep a fresh approach. They're better educated in music today, and they have all the experience that the older guys amassed to fall back on. I wouldn't tell any section of the band, "Do it this way." But I might say, "Don't do that, try it another way, is there another way you might like to try it."

When we would do our old tunes, we tried to stretch out and have individual players add their own concepts. How much room I gave someone on a tune depended on the player.

I would extend anybody's solo if they had something to say.

Sometimes the whole pattern of an oldie would change. In the case of "Woodchopper's Ball," we developed so many versions that we had to send out and get a stock arrangement to see how the thing was done to begin with. I think it's part of growing and living.

John Fedchock, the trombonist who played and arranged for the band from 1980 to 1987, recalls:

Woody didn't like to do the old stuff, and sometimes he would get bugged when people would request it.

One time at an old dance hall in Iowa, some guy who had a little too much to drink was angry that we weren't playing all the old hits. We weren't playing Glenn Miller, we weren't playing Tommy Dorsey, everything wasn't two-beat, he couldn't sing along. He went up to Woody and they exchanged words. Then I heard Woody say something like, "What did it cost you to get in here?" The guy told him, and Woody just whipped out a twenty and gave it to him, and said, "See you later, pal."

I started on the same day as Mike Brignola and John Oddo and a trumpet player, Steve Harrow. I took the place of Nelson Hines. I had been at the Eastman School of Music in Rochester, New York, doing master's work, and I met a few people there who knew some of Woody's players who had gone to Eastman. We went out to hear the band a couple of times and I gave a tape to Gene Smith, who was then the lead trombone player. When Nelson left the band, they gave me a call. As a matter of fact, it was about four in the morning, while they were in California playing Disneyland.

I got an official leave of absence from school and it worked out great. I returned in 1985 while Woody was doing a small group tour, and I squeezed everything I had left to do in five months. When the band went back out in May, I took a week off from school, joined them for some important gigs, and returned to school for my finals.

My first gig with the band was in Chicago—a three-hour concert in a park. I can't remember why, but I didn't have any chance to warm up all day. We went straight to the gig, and I had something like six solos that night. Nelson, the guy I replaced, played a lot of plunger and real funky type stuff. I knew how he played, but I figured I'd do my thing.

At the end of the evening, Woody came over to me and he was really angry. He said, "It's not funky enough. It's gotta be funkier or we'll have to do something about it." Here's this guy I always revered, this legend I always wanted to play with . . . It could have really made me apprehensive and nervous. Instead, it got me pissed off. I knew I could do what he wanted. It's just that I didn't know what he wanted before then.

The next night, I just bluesed out on every solo—I played every blues lick I'd ever learned or heard—and tried to make it swing real hard. Woody came up to me later that night, when we were hanging out at a bar, and said, "Sounds good." He just wanted to see if I had the roots for it. From then on, I was able to play however I wanted. It was on that second gig that he dubbed me Too Tall John, and he continued to call me that every night. Afterward, guys came up to me and said, "He must really like you, because he doesn't do that for everybody." Things were great from then on.

I did about sixteen or seventeen charts for Woody, but I didn't write for the band at first. I had taken one year of beginning arranging at Eastman. I had written one or two charts in my life. John Oddo had sort of taken over the writing chores in the band and I was apprehensive to even try. With this great band that I always wanted to play with, with all the great charts that had been recorded, I was more concerned with playing.

After about two-and-a-half years, I tried a chart. We were in the club in New Orleans for six months and I had an apartment. I figured it was a good time to do one. I wrote an arrangement on a Lou Donaldson tune called "Fried Buzzard." It featured Mike Brignola on baritone sax and myself. Woody said, "Maybe you ought to write it so that the melody is just unison saxophones." I didn't want to do that because there are three or four other charts in the book like that.

If I wrote it that way, he'd probably call those other charts. I stuck to my guns and he was cool about it. He started calling it every night. We recorded it later on the fiftieth anniversary album.

It was about eight months before I tried another. I was just sort of feeling my way around. The luxury was that every night you're playing great stuff and you're getting a feel for what voicings sound good. Also, the charts in Woody's book are paced very well; from beginning to end they have a nice shape to them. When you're studying in school, sometimes you don't get that because you're too worried about the mechanics; you lose the overall. But just playing that music night after night, you get a feel for the phrasing, for how much rest you need to leave for a brass section after you give them a hard blow.

The second chart was an original called "The Great Escape," which we recorded on the "Woody's Gold Star" album. It didn't go over as well as the first. We used it on jazz gigs, but not at dances. Then, after John Oddo had left the band, Woody said he wanted me to write something. I was all excited. My first assignment from Woody Herman. Later, at a private party for us after a gig in Baton Rouge, Louisiana, Woody said, "I want you to write a new funky version of Herbie Hancock's 'Watermelon Man.'"

That was the last thing I wanted to hear. There was already a "Watermelon Man" chart in the book by Nat Pierce. It was a funky jazz thing that the band recorded in the sixties. I really didn't want to update that. The guys were giving me a hard time about it because I was trying to let it lay. But Woody wouldn't let up. Every night he'd say, "You working on that chart? 'Cause I got some ideas for it." I finally decided to write it, and it came out OK. But it took a couple of years before he was comfortable with it because, as soon as I wrote it, he said it wasn't what he expected. I thought of funk in the modern sense, and he thought of funk as real bluesy. He had us add a trumpet solo at the beginning in kind of the old feel. He did that to a lot of charts.

On some of the older charts in the book, he might add a chorus of melody or add a chorus of rhythm in front, or just four bars in front. He wasn't really an arranger, per se, but he had the ears for it.

On his very last recording date, we had some Latin percussion players, and Woody said he wanted to try the "Watermelon Man" chart. The percussion players couldn't read music, so while I played my parts I'd be standing to wave them in or wave them out of passages. It was wild. I was almost a nervous wreck. But it came off great, and Woody was adamant about putting it on the album.

Woody never told us in advance what tunes we would play. But the band would know what the upcoming number was after a couple of words of the little rap he gave the audience. When he'd say, "Here's something from 1948," you knew it was "Early Autumn"; or something to feature the four saxophones, you knew it was "Four Brothers."

Woody would ride on the bus occasionally, but he didn't interact too much with the guys. He'd hang out in the bar after the gig sometimes. His only rule was to get on the stand and swing and play great. That was it.

There was always that sort of thing where guys were afraid to approach him. It wasn't like just talking to another guy in the band. He was sort of set up a little higher. On the bandstand, even though he wouldn't say anything, you could tell from how he was looking at someone in the band if he wasn't digging it. There were times when he might have been thinking only about the next tune, but if he happened to be looking in your direction, you were playing for Woody. Sal Nistico told me in 1984 that he still got nervous with Woody watching him. If he really liked your playing, you'd play more, be featured in concerts. If he didn't like the way you played, he wouldn't call tunes that you played on. There were occasions when he didn't like the way someone played a solo, so he'd open up the tune and bring down a guy he liked. On "Woodchopper's Ball," for instance, someone would come down front to play the solo. If Woody didn't dig it, he'd bring forward a second guy to play it, just to show the first guy "Hey, you're not making it." He didn't have to say anything.

We once played a huge dance in Canada for the Sylvania company, in a big hotel ballroom. It was obvious that this engagement was paying a lot of money. One of the guys from the company requested "Tie a Yellow Ribbon." At any other place, Woody would have had this guy beheaded. But Woody knew that this was one of the guys paying for the gig. The trouble was Woody didn't know the tune. He turned to the rhythm section and asked if anyone knew it, and they shrugged their shoulders. Then he turned to the rest of us, and none of us would have wanted to play it even if we knew it. The reason is that you have this great book lying in front of you and you're wasting five minutes of playing time.

Finally Woody said, "Fifty dollars to whoever will play 'Tie a Yellow Ribbon.'" Dave Riekenberg, the tenor player, stood up and played it. The rhythm section was kind of iffing it through the changes. Dave made fifty bucks.

At a policemen's ball outside of Boston, nobody was really listening to the band. We were positioned sort of off to the side, background music. Nobody cared that it was Woody Herman, living legend, up on the stage. As the night wore on, one of the guys in the band broke out a whoopee cushion, and started screwing around with it. When somebody went up for a solo, the cushion was on his seat when he returned. Eventually Woody started getting into it, and he would motion to put the whoopee cushion on somebody's seat.

The party was winding down, people were leaving, nobody was listening. Steve Harrow went out to play some blues on "Cousins," with a Harmon mute. Woody sent one of the guys up to the microphone with the whoopee cushion to trade fours with Steve. And Steve started making those same kinds of sounds with the horn. The band was roaring. But nobody was listening.

I started digging Woody's band when I was a junior in high school in Cleveland. The band actually came to my school to do a clinic and concert. It really made an impact; it was one of the things that helped me decide to go into music—wanting to play on that band, and to play trombone as well as Jim Pugh. It was inspiring. I sat in the front row, and got everyone's autograph on a record that I still have.

That's when I really started collecting the Woody Herman records and getting into all the charts. When I came on the band, I had two or three ninety-minute cassettes full of anything that Woody might call. So as far as reading the book when I got there, I even had some of my parts memorized. I knew on certain tunes where the trombone section had to stand up and play a passage. Reading the arrangements wasn't any worry for me.

The thing I always noticed about Woody's playing—especially after being on the band for a while and then looking at old films and listening to the old records—was that he really swung. Even when he was playing with minimum chops and minimum ideas, everything felt good. Every other clarinet player is so preoccupied with what notes he's playing and how many he can play. But Woody's main thing was swinging. Even if he just played something simple, it would come off because it really felt good. That came off in the band; you'd pick up on it. Woody's swing feel was something I have yet to find in another clarinet player. It was very relaxed, very flowing.

We did an album with clarinetist Richard Stolzman, and I wrote a chart on "Come Sunday" for Richard to play. The chart builds up at the end; I wrote it so that he would play over the band, the way Woody did. He had a heck of a time relating to the concept of having to play over this massive sound with just a clarinet. His manager said, "You can't do that with a clarinet." Mike Brignola said, "Well, you better talk to Woody, 'cause he does it every night."

Woody once asked Byron Stripling, who was our lead trumpet player at the time, to play a high G at the end of "Things Ain't What They Used To Be." Byron said, "I'll give it a try." And Woody replied, "Well, if you can do it, I can still top you by a third."

I always wanted our material to come from within the band, which is why I sought pieces from my players. That was the secret of our freshness. And that's why I always told interviewers that my favorite herd was the one I'd have next year.

We always had guys in the band who would write charts, from the beginning. I felt that the most constructive way to write was for a certain group of musicians. If you could make those guys become profound as soloists with what you wrote as background for them, it was a stepping-stone for the players and the writers alike.

Besides Joe Bishop, Ralph Burns, Neal Hefti, Al Cohn, and Nat Pierce, there was always someone who contributed. Jimmy Rowles didn't do charts for me, but he always had great suggestions about tunes and ideas.

When I needed something, there was Bill Holman. I rarely requested a chart, but usually someone would do something and bring it in. Gary Anderson did many great things for us— "Fanfare for the Common Man" and "Don't You Worry 'Bout a Thing." He came out of Berklee and has since done everything from movie work to television.

And, of course, there was Alan Broadbent and John Fedchock. David LaLama was another pianist who could take direction very well. He was very important to the band, and Alan Broadbent, in the seventies. I would tell him what I needed and he would do it.

With writers like that, and the kinds of players we managed to find and help develop, I never considered myself a bandleader. I was a coach.

21
ANYPLACE I
HANG MY HAT

The Internal Revenue Service was getting the lion's share of our earnings. But few people were aware of it, aside from close friends. I refused to go public with it while Charlotte was alive. She was fiercely proud, and there was no point in causing embarrassment.

I managed to live very well on the road, taking enough expense money as I needed to ensure good accommodations and good meals. But I was also keenly aware that it would end if we missed a payment to the government every week. We'd be out of business, without any material goods other than the house and the clothes on my back.

Suddenly, in 1985, my ownership of the house was in jeopardy as well. The government notified me that it would be auctioned off to help satisfy the tax debt.

It all happened with little fanfare. I feel there wasn't

enough public notice, and that only certain people knew about it. If you were into buying properties, I guess you could find out easily. The person who wound up with it, William Little, was apparently doing a lot of business with the government on properties.

Little got the house for 99,000 some-odd dollars—an astoundingly low price, considering that we had a legitimate estimate that the house was worth around $350,000. I presented the government with the fact that my wife and I had signed a will leaving the house to Ingrid. Charlotte's death, in effect, had given Ingrid half of the house. The document, however, had been drawn up during the last few days of Charlotte's life, and the government apparently doesn't like last-minute wills. After much fighting, it was decided that Ingrid owned 50 percent of the house and that 50 percent of the purchase price paid by Little was to be held in escrow for her. But she wouldn't pick up the money because we were still trying to work out something to make it possible to keep the house.

An arrangement was negotiated in which we would pay rent to Little for half of the house—a home that I had paid cash for almost forty years earlier. Only the government could have thought of something like that.

When the public learned of the situation concerning my debt and the status of my home, I tried to gloss over it with humor. "Having the IRS in on my house has fringe benefits," I said. "One IRS guy shows up twice a week to mow the lawn. Another one cleans and trims the bushes."

But I was not amused. Being a man without credit was difficult enough for me, and I had been in that position for more than twenty years. I had to have cash on me at all times. I was without a personal bank account or credit cards—a tough existence for a man constantly on the road. I usually had to pay my hotel bills in advance.

I figured that, with the visits I had made to other parts

of the world for the State Department, they might at least leave me something to hang my hat on. The government had put liens on everything I had touched. I felt that I should be looked upon as a human being who had tried very hard to be correct.

But I didn't expect any miracles. If the IRS had taken some of the rigor mortis off me, there were lots of things I wanted to do, such as be able to pay for a vacation in which I wasn't confined to the home I was in danger of losing.

Those problems, however, didn't affect the music we were playing or my desire to continue playing it. I was able to shunt off a lot of stuff because of the way I was educated. The schools did a good job of teaching me a philosophy of staying alive, which is why I have never truly been depressed.

Just when I was becoming accustomed to being a tenant in my own home, William Little informed us of his intention to sell the place and of our need to vacate. But a judge granted us a six-month extension to remain and, meanwhile, my lawyer was attempting to resolve the situation. Ingrid, who had followed Hermie Dressel as the band's business manager in 1981, was certainly not about to give up the house for half of $99,000.

22
THE CODA

I was weary. It became harder each day to gather strength for another hike to another town, to another hotel room, to another guy asking me, "Hey, Mr. Herman, how do you like it here in Decatur?" or wherever the hell we were.

On the bandstand, things were fine, we were swinging. Tom Cassidy, our booker, was keeping us busy; Bill Byrne, our road manager, was taking care of details; and trombonist/arranger John Fedchock and Frank Tiberi, who had been an anchor in the sax section for many years, were keeping our music fresh and exciting.

But off the stage I was dragging my ass. Most of the time, I couldn't remember where we had played yesterday. I still loved the music, but being reduced to a government serf was gnawing at me.

We nonetheless had a reason to celebrate. It was 1986, my fiftieth year in front of a band. We hadn't merely survived the collapse of the big band era, the crush of rock and roll, and a twenty-year income-tax battle which kept me at the brink of poverty. We had also managed to keep the music adventurous and ensured the requisite energy by keeping the ranks filled with energetic and talented young men.

Fifty years called for a helluva celebration.

Through George Simon, meanwhile, I had met and heard a great young classical clarinetist named Richard Stolzman, who was to play a key role in the anniversary concert we were preparing.

George Simon recalls:

I met Richard Stolzman on the West Coast sometime in the early eighties at the Grammy Awards, and he told me that he loved to play jazz. I told him, "Why don't you sit in with us sometime at Twilight Jazz," which was the early evening gig I was doing with writer Bill Simon and other musicians each Wednesday in New York. At that time we were installed at Eddie Condon's.

One Tuesday, I came home and listened to my answering machine. One of the messages was a voice that said, "Mr. Simon, this is Richard Stolzman. I play the clarinet. When we met in Los Angeles, you said some time when I came to New York I might be able to sit in with your group. I'd love to come in tomorrow evening. But if you don't want me to, just put a sign outside that says to stay away."

I called him back and he came in. And so did Woody Herman.

Richard Stolzman recalls:

I played a little blues and one reckless chorus of "Take the A-Train." Then George said to me, "There's somebody over in the corner who wants to talk to you."

I couldn't believe it—Woody Herman.

He talked to me about my playing and asked if I were interested in playing "Ebony Concerto" with his band at the fiftieth anniversary concert at the Hollywood Bowl.

I had first heard the piece when I was in college, and I wasn't particularly impressed with it. I guess I thought at that time that I was going to hear a jazz piece and, when I didn't, I ignored it. Later on, I learned that the sounds, harmonizations, voice leadings, and such in the piece were really special—jazzlike and ahead of their time. Stravinsky had a fondness sometimes for rather reckless intervals, odd leaps, and kind of jagged, quirky lines. But after having played "Ebony" many times, it seems to me to be exactly right.

The fiftieth anniversary concert, on July 16, 1987, was a highly emotional day for me. Between the rigors of assembling the program, I was preoccupied constantly with thoughts of my parents, of Charlotte, and of Sister Fabian, who had given me support in school—all those who had been as incremental in feeding my musical fire as Duke Ellington.

Finally, there was the music itself, lush and punchy, delivered by the herd and a second band, packed with alumni: Pete and Conte Candoli, Bill Berry, Don Rader, and John Audino on trumpets; Dick Hyde, Buster Cooper, and Carl Fontana on trombones; Dick Hafer, Med Flory, Bob Cooper, Jack Nimitz, and Herman Riley on saxes, and a rhythm section of Nat Pierce, Monty Budwig, and Chuck Flores.

More than 12,000 people heard us play not just the expected revivals—"Blowin' Up a Storm," "Bijou"—but a new composition that Ralph Burns wrote in honor of Charlotte, called "Godmother." Rosemary Clooney sang "My Buddy," and Jimmy Rowles, with his daughter Stacy on flugelhorn, were elegant on "Old Folks" and Billy Strayhorn's "Lotus Blossom." Rowles returned for a duet with Stan Getz, playing Jimmy's "Peacocks," which they had recorded years earlier.

Before Richard Stolzman came out to play "Ebony Concerto," I told the audience: "Since we first played this piece at Carnegie Hall forty years ago, I have been hoping and wanting dearly to hear it—particularly my solo—as it should be played."

Then I took a seat on the stage.

Stolzman gave it the kind of justice a work of art deserves.

At the end of the concert, the party continued through the night at my home with a couple of hundred friends.

Two days later, the band was back to business as usual. But my body wasn't. Pain from the steel pin in my leg made walking a hardship. It was difficult to get through an airplane terminal or to climb stairs. Just the thought of packing and unpacking, of hopping from hotel to hotel, from city to tank town, was awesome.

For the first time, I looked for help, and I found it in Ed Dye, who began accompanying me on the road as valet, aide, nurse, and general man Friday. But the fatigue of living on the road was relentless, like the tax and house problems. The nightly music was the only payoff and my failing health was making it difficult to perform for more than an hour. By November 1986, while playing an engagement outside of New York City, I collapsed and was taken to Bellevue Hospital in Manhattan, where they pumped at least a pint of water from my lungs. Lying in a crowded hospital ward didn't make for much of a Thanksgiving.

Stuart Troup recalls:

Woody lay in bed in a noisy ward when I arrived with Polly Podewell, the singer who had performed with him from time to time during the previous few years.

He looked more frail than usual. In a weak voice, he admitted that his body wasn't up to what little spirit he had left. Just before I was leaving, he smiled, took my hand, and motioned for me to come closer.

"You know," he said, "Igor Stravinsky was right. He said that growing old is just a series of humiliations."

Frank Tiberi fronted the band in my place. When I left

the hospital, I went to Jack and Mary Siefert's home outside of Philadelphia to recuperate.

I rejoined the band after a few weeks, but my energy was minimal. I don't know how I put together the strength to record early in March 1987, when we made the *Woody's Gold Star* album for Concord.

Shortly afterward, we played an engagement in Denver, and the altitude was getting to me. I got some medicine for it, but I felt noticeably weaker.

John Fedchock recalls:

In Denver, Woody started to get really sick. Some of the decisions about the Gold Star album hadn't been made yet—we just had the rough tapes—and he told me, "Come by my room tomorrow and we'll talk about the record and decide what to do." I went up to his room at about four in the afternoon. He answered the door in his underwear, and his hair was sticking up all over the place. He had been in bed all day, and he said, "Sorry, all I can do is sleep." He wanted to conserve his energy for the two hours of playing each night. I remember him sitting down very slowly in a chair next to the desk, and he said, "OK, what have we got here?"

I showed him a piece of paper with the names of the tunes, but he had trouble reading it, so I read it to him. He said, "I want to make sure that they put some extra tunes on the CD." That was very important to him. If someone was going to spend the extra money for a CD, he wanted to give them something extra.

About three weeks later he went into the hospital in Detroit, and they said that he had only about 25 percent of his lung capacity. So he played on that last album date with virtually no air. And he still sounded good.

After the Denver engagement, the tour took us to Grand Meadow, Minn., for a concert at the high school. By the end of the evening, I had nothing left. The next stop was Dr. Stan Levy in Detroit.

EPILOGUE

Woody was hospitalized in Detroit. "Dr. Stan Levy worked on him around the clock," Jack Siefert said. "He practically gave up his private practice."

His body was under attack from emphysema and heart disease, and his health continued to fail after months in the Detroit hospital. After a transfer to Cedars-Sinai Medical Center in Los Angeles for several weeks, he went home to his Hollywood Hills bedroom for a while, where he remained tied to a life-support system, with oxygen, a wheelchair and a nurse at his bedside. His daughter, Ingrid, and singer Polly Podewell tried to comfort him, but his periods of consciousness and coherence kept diminishing. He had to return to the hospital several times.

With his lungs and his heart becoming increasingly weak,

Woody was taken again to Cedars-Sinai, where he died on October 29, 1987.

Four days later, at ten o'clock in the morning, Jack Seifert was a solitary figure sitting in a forward pew at St. Victor's Catholic Church in West Hollywood—the same church in which a funeral mass was celebrated for Charlotte five years earlier. He was composing a eulogy when he was interrupted by my arrival. He knew that Woody and I were writing a book, but we had never met. We had a couple of hours before the funeral was to begin, and we talked, first at the church and then over a snack at a nearby restaurant.

"Woody was not a gift-wrapped empty box," Jack said. "He was a modest musician, never a wiseguy. And he had a fantastic sense of humor."

I told him how one night, while Woody and I were taping some history at our usual corner in a Manhattan lounge, someone began to play the spinet piano. My back was to it, and the sound came as a shock, since I had never seen anyone go near the piano before. The player, obviously aware of Woody's presence, was delivering a feeble reading of "Early Autumn."

"What the hell is this?" I said.

Woody was somber-faced, but with a twinkle in his eyes—the look that often preceded one of his droll remarks. He said, "They have a song demonstrator here."

"He had a special way of phrasing everything," Jack responded. "If he addressed someone as 'pal,' for instance, you knew he had no use for the guy."

I remembered Woody using that term the first time I met him, in 1945, after the band had just finished a matinee performance at a Broadway theater. I was eleven and couldn't afford to go inside, but I was among a group of about fifteen awaiting Woody at the stage door. When he appeared, autograph books were thrust toward him. I was smaller than the others, and last.

Long before he got to my book, an insistent fan began

noisily elbowing others out of the way. Woody looked up from the book he was signing and said, "What's your problem, pal?" His inflection reduced the bully to a lamb.

"C'mere, kid," Herman called to me. I gave him my book and, as he was writing, he said, "You know your way around the city?" I nodded.

"Want to do me a favor?"

Holy mackerel, sure. He took out a piece of paper, wrote a note, and stuffed it into an envelope. "Take this over to the Lincoln Hotel on Eighth Avenue," he said. "It's for Horace Heidt."

Woody reached into a pocket and gave me a five-dollar bill, a fortune for a kid in 1945.

Thirty-seven years later, while sitting at a rehearsal in Fat Tuesday's in Manhattan, I asked him, "Why did you give me so much?"

"I was trying to make a paying customer out of you," he replied.

A crowd was gathering when Jack and I returned to the church. Among Woody's friends were Henry Mancini, Les Brown, Ray Anthony, and Stan Kenton's widow, Audrey. Gene Lees was chatting with members of Woody's alumni, who included Ralph Burns, Jimmy Rowles, Nat Pierce, Bill Holman, Ross Tompkins, Bill Perkins, Cappy Lewis—whose trumpet was heard on the original recording of "Woodchopper's Ball"—and Cappy's son Mark, who became a second-generation trumpet player in the band; Mary Ann McCall, John Fedchock, Terry Gibbs, Pete Candoli, Don Rader, Dave Riekenberg, and others.

Ingrid arrived with her children, Polly Podewell, and Charlotte's mother, Inga Neste.

Only trumpeter Bill Byrne was there to represent the then-current Herman Herd. The band, he explained, was on the road, having played a concert the night before at Oklahoma State University, with Frank Tiberi leading.

"Woody wanted a simple, traditional mass," Jack said, "in tribute to his parents." Monsignor George Parnassus complied after the carnation-and-rose-covered casket was wheeled down the center aisle.

"Woody, the one word that means so much to so many," Jack Siefert intoned to the two hundred or so assembled mourners. "As a bandleader, he defied the laws of physics because of his unique talent of being able to make the whole greater than the sum of its parts. . . . Above all, he was a role model for the young people of today, for he proved that you can still reach your artistic goals and be a nice guy. . . . Woody was the rarest of all human possessions: he was a true friend."

Jack's eulogy was brief and particularly poignant when he summoned the words to "Early Autumn." The appropriateness was astonishing.

"Woody always felt that Johnny Mercer was one of America's greatest poets," he said, and he began to read:

When an early autumn walks the land
And chills the breeze,
And touches with her hand
The summer trees,
Perhaps you'll understand
What memories
I own.
There's a dance pavilion in the rain
All shuttered down,
A winding country lane
All russet brown,
A frosted windowpane
Shows me a town
Grown lonely . . .

SELECTED
DISCOGRAPHY

ABBREVIATIONS:

(as)	alto saxophone	(g)	guitar
(b)	string bass	(p)	piano
(bs)	baritone sax	(pc)	percussion
(btp)	bass trumpet	(ss)	soprano sax
(cga)	conga drums	(tb)	trombone
(cl)	clarinet	(tp)	trumpet
(cls)	celeste	(ts)	tenor sax
(d)	drums	(v)	vocal
(eb)	electric bass	(vb)	vibraphone
(ep)	electric piano	(vn)	violin
(f)	flute	(ww)	woodwinds
(flh)	flugelhorn		

U.S.:	United States release
U.K.:	United Kingdom release
Fr.:	French release

WOODY HERMAN RARE LIVE BROADCASTS
Brooklyn Roseland and others

Sunbeam, SB 206
11/8/36

Blue Prelude, Liza, Royal Garden Blues, Rose Room, The Goose Hangs High, Medley, Basin Street Blues, Jazz Me Blues, Lullaby in Rhythm, Rosetta, Time Changes Everything, Danciing in the Dark, I Ain't Got Nobody, Yardbird Suite, Bishop's Blues, Blues in the Night.

BEST OF WOODY HERMAN

MCA, 2-4077
4/12/38 11/8/43

THE TURNING POINT

U.S. MCA Decca DL9229
U.K., Coral CP2
11/43 12/44

Basie's Basement, Do Nothin' Till You Hear From Me, I Get a Kick Out of You, Crying Sands, I'll Get By, I've Got You Under My Skin, Noah, Cherry, Milkman Keep Those Bottles Quiet, It Must Be Jelly Cause Jam Don't Shake Like That, Ingie Speaks, Perdido, As Long as I Live, I Ain't Got Nothin' But the Blues.

On *Do Nothin' Till You Hear From Me, Down Under:* Ray Wetzel, Bobby Guyer, Benny Stabler, Nick Travis, Cappy Lewis (tp), Al Mastren, Ed Kiefer, Eddie Bert (tb), Woody Herman (cl, as, v), Johnny Bothwell, Chuck DiMaggio (as), Pete Mondello, Ben Webster (ts), Skippy DeSair (bs), Dick Kane (p), Hy White (g), Chubby Jackson (b), Cliff Leeman (d).

On *Noah, I've Got You Under My Skin, I Get a Kick Out of You, I'll Get By, Crying Sands:* Omit Benny Stabler, add Allen Eager (ts), Ralph Burns (p) replaces Dick Kane.

On *Cherry, Milkman Keep Those Bottles Quiet, It Must Be Jelly...:* Ray Wetzel, Bobby Guyer, Mario Serritello, Neal Hefti (tp), Ed Kiefer, Ed Bennett, Al Esposito (tb), Woody Herman (cl, as, v), Ernie Caceres, Chuck DiMaggio (as), Pete Mondello, Budd Johnson (ts), Skippy DeSair (bs), Ralph Burns (p), Hy White (g), Marjorie Hyams (vb), Chubby Jackson (b), Cliff Leeman (d), Frances Wayne (v).

On *Ingie Speaks:* Nick Travis (tp) and Georgie Auld (ts) replace Neal Hefti and Budd Johnson.

On *Perdido:* Ray Wetzel, Billy Robbins, Mario Serritello, Ray Nance, Neal Hefti (tp), Ed Kiefer, Al Esposito, Juan Tizol (tb), Woody Herman (cl, as, v), Chuck DiMaggio, Johnny Hodges (as), Pete Mondello, Herbie Fields (ts), Skippy DeSair (bs), Ralph Burns (p), Billy Bauer (g), Chubby Jackson (b), Red Saunders (d).

On *As Long as I Live, I Ain't Got Nothin' But the Blues:* Ray Wetzel, Dick Munson, Conte Candoli, Pete Candoli, Neal Hefti (tp), Ed Kiefer, Ralph Pfeffner, Bill Harris (tb), Woody Herman (cl, as, v), Sam Marowitz, Bill Shine (as), Pete Mondello, Flip Phillips (ts), Skippy DeSair (bs), Ralph Burns (p), Billy Bauer (g), Chubby Jackson (b), Dave Tough (d), Frances Wayne (v).

WOODY HERMAN AND HIS FIRST HERD 1944
The Old Gold Radio Shows

U.S. Hindsight HSR 134
U.K. HMA 5058
8/2/43 10/4/44

Is You Is or Is You Ain't My Baby, It Must Be Jelly Cause Jam Don't Shake

Like That, Red Top, Sweet Lorraine, G.I. Jive, Jones Beachhead, Four or Five Times, Blues on Parade, 125th Street Prophet, Somebody Loves Me, Basie's Basement, There'll Be a Hot Time in the Town of Berlin, 1-2-3-4 Jump, Apple Honey.

On *It Must Be Jelly..., G.I. Jive, Red Top, Blues on Parade, Jones Beachhead, Four or Five Times:* Same personnel as on Perdido in previous album.

On *125th Street Prophet, Somebody Loves Me, Basie's Basement, There'll Be a Hot Time..., Sweet Lorraine, Is You Is...:* Carl Warwick, Chuck Frankhauser (tp) and John La Porta (as) replace Duck Munson, Conte Candoli and Bill Shine.

On *1-2-3-4 Jump:* The Woodchoppers, with Herman (cl), Neal Hefti (tp), Bill Harris (tb), Flip Phillips (ts), Marjorie Hyams (vb), Ralph Burns (p), Billy Bauer (g), Chubby Jackson (b), Dave Tough (d).

On *Apple Honey:* Same personnel as on 125th Street Prophet.

WOODY HERMAN GREATEST HITS

CBS CS9291

1945-46

Apple Honey, The Good Earth, Woodchopper's Ball, Your Faather's Moustache, Blue Flame, Northwest Passage, Caldonia, Summer Sequence (part 4), Bijou, Four Brothers, Wild Root.

Exact personnel unavailable.

THE THREE HERDS 1945-1954

CBS JCL 592

1945-54

Non-Alcoholic, Caldonia, Sidewalks of Cuba, The Good Earth, Four Brothers, The Goof and I, Keen and Peachy, Early Autumn, Four Others, Blame Boehm, Mulligan Tawny, The Third Herd.

Exact personnel unavailable.

WOODY HERMAN: THE THUNDERING HERDS (3-RECORD SET)

U.S. CBSC3L25

U.K. CBS-BPG62160-59-60

4/45 12/27/47

Summer Sequence (1st 3 parts), Everywhere, With Someone New, Wrap Your Troubles in Dreams, Back Talk, Non-Alcoholic, I Told Ya I Love Ya Now Get Out, I've Got News for You, Keen and Peachy, The Goof and I, Lazy Lullaby, Four Brothers, Summer Sequence (part 4), P.S. I Love You.

On *Wrap Your Troubles in Dreams, P.S. I Love You:* Mary Ann McCall (v).

On *Summer Sequence, Everywhere, With Someone New, Wrap Your Troubles in Dreams, Back Talk:* Conrad Gozzo, Cappy Lewis, Shorty Rogers, Pete Candoli, Sonny Berman (tp), Ed Kiefer, Ralph Pfeffner, Neil Reid, Bill Harris (tb), Woody Herman (cl, as), Sam Marowitz, John La Porta (as), Mickey Folus, Flip Phillips (ts), Sam Rubinwitch (bs), Red Norvo (vb), Ralph Burns (p), Chuck

Wayne (g), Joe Mondragon (b), Don Lamond (d), Mary Ann McCall (v).

On *Non-Alcoholic:* Conrad Gozzo, Chuck Peterson, Cappy Lewis, Al Porcino, Bob Peck (tp), Ed Kiefer, Ralph Pfeffner, Bill Harris (tb), Woody Herman (cl), Sam Marowitz, John La Porta (as), Flip Phillips (ts), Sam Rubinwitch (bs), Jimmy Rowles (p), Chuck Wayne (g), Joe Mondragon (b), Don Lamond (d).

On *I Told Ya I Love Ya, Now Get Out, I've Got News for You, Keen and Peachy, The Goof and I, Lazy Lullaby, Four Brothers, Summer Sequence (part 4):* Bernie Glow, Stan Fishelson, Irvin Markowitz, Shorty Rogers, Ernie Royal (tp), Ollie Wilson, Earl Swope, Bob Swift (tb), Woody Herman (cl, as, v), Sam Marowitz (as), Herbie Steward (ts, as), Stan Getz, Zoot Sims (ts), Serge Chaloff (bs), Fred Otis and Ralph Burns on last 4 titles (p), Gene Sargent (g), Walter Yoder (b), Don Lamond (d), Mary Ann McCall (v).

On *P.S. I Love You:* Al Cohn (ts) and Jimmy Raney (g) replace Herbie Steward and Gene Sargent.

WOODY HERMAN FIRST HERD AT CARNEGIE HALL VOL. I & II

U.S. Verve VSP1 & VSP26
U.K. Verve 2317 031
3/25/46

Red Top, Bijou, Mean to Me, Your Father's Moustache, Blowin' Up a Storm, Sweet and Lovely, Everywhere, Panacea, The Good Earth, Four Men on a Horse, The Man I Love, Superman With a Horn, Heads Up, Hallelujah, Wild Root.

Conrad Gozzo, Irvin Markowitz, Shorty Rogers, Pete Candoli, Sonny Berman (tp), Ed Kiefer, Ralph Pfeffner, Bill Harris (tb), Woody Herman (cl, as, v), Sam Marowitz, John La Porter (as), Mickey Folus, Flip Phillips (ts), Sam Rubinwitch (bs), Red Norvo (vb), Tony Aless (p), Billy Bauer (g), Chubby Jackson (b), Don Lamond (d).

WOODY HERMAN: EARLY AUTUMN

Capitol-EMI M11034
1948-50

That's Right, Lemon Drop, Early Autumn, Keeper of the Flame, More Moon, Lollypop, Not Really the Blues, Tenderly, Rhapsody in Wood, Music to Dance To, Sonny Speaks, Starlight Souvenirs, The Great Lie.

On *Lemon Drop, That's Right, Early Autumn, Keeper of the Flame:* Bernie Glow, Stan Fishelson, Irvin Markowitz, Shorty Rogers, Ernie Royal (tp), Ollie Wilson, Earl Swope, Bill Harris, Bob Swift (tb), Woody Herman (cl, as, v), Sam Marowitz (as), Al Cohn, Stan Getz, Zoot Sims (ts), Serge Chaloff (bs), Terry Gibbs (vb), Lou Levy (p), Chubby Jackson (b), Don Lamond (d), Mary Ann McCall (v), scat bop vocal by Rogers, Gibbs and Jackson.

On *More Moon:* Al Porcino, Stan Fishelson, Charlie Walp, Shorty Rogers, Ernie Royal (tp), Ollie Wilson, Earl Swope, Bill Harris, Bart Varsalona (tb), Woody Herman (cl, as), Sam Marowitz (as), Jimmy Giuffre, Gene Ammons,

Buddy Savitt (ts), Serge Chaloff (bs), Terry Gibbs (vb), Lou Levy (p), Oscar Pettiford (b), Shelley Manne (d).

On *Not Really the Blues, Lollypop, Tenderly, Rhapsody in Wood, The Great Lie:* Joe Mondragon (b) replaces Oscar Pettiford.

On *Lollypop:* Scat bop vocal by Rogers, Gibbs and Herman.

On *Music to Dance To, Sonny Speaks:* Don Ferrara, Rolf Ericson, Doug Mettome, Conte Candoli (tp), Herb Randel, Jerry Dorn, Bill Harris (tb), Woody Herman (cl, as), Phil Urso, Buddy Wise, Bob Graf (ts), Marty Flax (bs), Dave McKenna (p), Red Mitchell (b), Sonny Igoe (d).

On *Starlight Souvenirs:* Vern Friley (tb) replaces Bill Harris.

HEY! HERD THE HERD? *French Issue Title: Men From Mars*

> U.S. Verve VG8558
> Fr. Verve 2304 509
> 7/7/52

Terrisita, Stompin' at the Savoy, Celestial Blues, Perdido, Moten Stomp, Blue Lou, Wooftie, Men From Mars, Four Others, Marakeesh, Castle Rock, Mambo the Most (parts 1 and 2).

On *Terrisita, Stompin' at the Savoy:* John Howell, Jack Scarda, Roy Caton, Don Fagerquist (tp), Jack Green, Carl Fontana, Urbie Green (tb), Woody Herman (cl, as), Dick Hafer, Arno Marsh, Bill Perkins (ts), Sam Staff (bs), Nat Pierce (p, cls), Chubby Jackson (b), Sonny Igoe (d).

On *Celestial Blues, Perdido, Moten Stomp:* Lee Fortier (tp) replaces Jack Scarda.

On *Blue Lou, Wooftie:* Phil Cook, Roy Caton, Tommy DiCarlo, Dick Sherman, Stu Williamson (tp), Jack Green, Will Bradley, Carl Fontana (tb), Woody Herman (cl), Dick Hafer, Arno Marsh, Bill Perkins (ts), Sam Staff (bs), Nat Pierce (p, cls), Chubby Jackson (b), Art Mardigan (d).

On *Men From Mars:* Joe Burnett, Roy Caton, Tommy DiCarlo, Stu Williamson (tp), Jack Green, Carl Fontana, Urbie Green (tb), Dick Hafer, Arno Marsh, Bill Trujillo (ts), Sam Staff (bs), Nat Pierce (p, organ), Red Kelly (b), Art Mardigan (d).

On *Four Brothers:* Bernie Glow, Ernie Royal, Harold Wegbreit, Bobby Styles, Stu Williamson (tp), Vern Friley, Urbie Green, Frank Rehak, Kai Winding (tb), Jerry Coker, Dick Hafer, Bill Trujillo (ts), Sam Staff (bs), Nat Pierce (p), Red Kelly (b), Art Madigan (d).

On *Marakeesh:* John Howell, Bernie Glow, Jim Bonebrake, Reuben McFall (tp), Dick Kenney, Jim Hewitt, Frank Rehak, Kai Winding (tb), Woody Herman (cl), Jerry Coker, Dick Hafer, Bill Trujillo (ts), Nat Pierce (p), Red Kelly (b), Art Mardigan (d).

On *Mambo the Most:* Al Porcino, John Howell, Bill Castagnino, Reuben McFall, Dick Collins (tp), Cy Touf (btp), Dick Kenney, Keith Moon (tb), Woody Herman (cl, as), Jerry Coker, Dick Hafer, Bill Perkins (ts), Jack Nimitz (bs), Nat Pierce (p), Red Kelly (b), Chuck Flores (d).

On *Castle Rock:* Sam Taylor (ts) and Mickey Baker (g) added; Lloyd Trotman (b) and Panama Francis (d) replace Red Kelly and Chuck Flores.

WOODY HERMAN: THE THIRD HERD VOL. I

Discovery DS815
5/30/52 9/11/53

Stompin' at the Savoy, Blues in Advance, Terissita, Moten Swing, No True Love, Go Down the Wisin' Road, Blue Lou I, Blue Lou II, I Love Paris, The Moon Is Blue.
   Exact personnel unavailable.

WOODY HERMAN: THE THIRD HERD VOL. II

Discovery DS 845
1952-54

Beau Jazz, Early Autumn, Mambo the Most, Mother Goose Jumps, Four Others, Buck Dance, Sorry 'Bout That Whole Darned Thing, Men From Mars, Wooftie.
   Exact personnel unavailable.

THE WOODY HERMAN BAND!

Capitol-EMI T560
9/54

Wild Apple Honey, Strange, Misty Morning, Would He?, Sleep, Autobahn Blues, By Play, La Cucaracha Mambo, Ill Wind, Boo Hoo, Hittin' the Bottle.
   Al Porcino, John Howell, Bill Castagnino, Charlie Walp, Dick Collins (tp), Cy Touff (btp), Dick Kenney, Keith Moon (tb), Woody Herman (cl, as), Dave Madden, Dick Hafer, Bill Perkins (ts) Jack Nimitz (bs), Nat Pierce (p), Red Kelly (b), Chuck Flores (d).

ROAD BAND!

U.S. Capitol-EMI T658
U.K. Capitol
(3 EP sides):
EAP 1009, 2-658, 3-658
10/13/54 6/6-7/55

Opus de Funk, Gina, I Remember Duke, Sentimental Journey, Cool Cat on a Hot Tin Roof, Where or When, Captain Ahab, I'll Never Be the Same, Pimlico.
   On *I'll Never Be the Same, Gina:* Same personnel as on previous album, except Richie Kamuca (ts) replaces Dave Madden.
   On *Opus de Funk, Cool Cat..., Pimlico:* Jerry Kail, Gerry LaFurn, Bernie Glow, Reuben McFall, Charlie Walp, Dick Collins (tp), Cy Touff (btp), Dick Kenney, Keith Moon (tb), Dick Hafer, Richie Kamuca, Art Pirie (ts), Jack Nimitz (bs), Nat Pierce (p), Billy Bauer (g), John Beal (b), Chuck Flores (d).

On *Captain Ahab, Remember Duke:* Nick Travis replaces Bernie Glow.
On *Sentimental Journey, Where or When:* Nick Travis omitted.

THE HERD RIDES AGAIN

U.S. Everest BR5003
U.K. Top Rank 35/038
7/30/58

*Northwest Passage, Caldonia, Wild Root, The Good Earth, Blowin' Up a
Storm, I Cover the Waterfront, It's Coolin' Time, Crazy Rhythm, Sinbad the
Sailor, Fire Island, Black Orchid, Bijou.*

Al Stewart, Bernie Glow, Nick Travis, Irvin Markowitz, Ernie Royal (tp),
Billy Byers, Frank Rehak, Bob Brookmeyer (tb), Woody Herman (cl, as, v), Sam
Marowitz (as), Al Cohn, Sam Donahue, Paul Quinichette (ts), Danny Bank (bs),
Nat Pierce (p), Billy Bauer (g), Chubby Jackson (b), Don Lamond (d).

On last six cuts: Burt Collins and Bernie Privin (tp) replace Bernie Glow and
Nick Travis.

WOODY HERMAN: 1963

U.S. Trip TLP5547
U.K. Philips 652 025
10/15-16/62

*Mo-Lasses, Blues for J.P., Don't Get Around Much Anymore, Tunin' In, Sis-
ter Sadie, Sig Ep, It's a Lonesome Old Town, Camel Walk.*

Bill Chase, Paul Fontaine, Ziggy Harrell, Dave Gale, Gerry Lamy (tp), Phil
Wilson, Eddie Morgan, Jack Gale (tb), Woody Herman (cl, as, v), Gordon
Brisker, Larry Cavelli, Sal Nistico (ts), Gene Allen (bs), Nat Pierce (p), Chuck
Andrus (b), Jake Hanna (d).

ENCORE: WOODY HERMAN - 1963

U.S. Trip TLP 5570
U.S. Philips PHM 200-0925
5/19-21/63

*That's Where It Is, Watermelon Man, Body and Soul, Better Get It in Your
Soul, Jazz Me Blues, El Toro Grande, Days of Wine and Roses, Caldonia.*

Bill Chase, Billy Hunt, Paul Fontaine, Dave Gale, Gerry Lamy (tp), Phil Wil-
son, Henry Southall, Bob Rudolph (tb), Woody Herman (cl, as, v), Bobby Jones,
Bill Perkins, Sal Nistico (ts), Frank Hitter (bs), Nat Pierce (p), Chuck Andrus (b),
Jake Hanna (d).

WOODY HERMAN - WOODY'S WINNERS

U.S. CBS CL 2436
U.K. CBS BPG62619
6/28-30/65

23 Red, My Funny Valentine, Northwest Passage, Poor Butterfly, Greasy

Sack Blues, Woody's Whistle, Red Roses for a Blue Lady, Opus de Funk, Blue Flame.

Bill Chase, Don Rader, Bobby Shew, Dusko Goykovich, Gerry Lamy (tp), Henry Southall, Frenk Tesinsky, Donald Doane (tb), Woody Herman (cl, as, ss), Gary Klein, Andy McGhee, Sal Nistico (ts), Tom Anastas (bs), Nat Pierce (p), Tony Leonardi (b), Ronnie Zito (d).

CONCERTO FOR HERD - MONTEREY

Verve V6 8764

9/67

Concerto for Herd I, II, III; Big Sur Echo, The Horn of the Fish, Woody's Boogaloo.

Exact personnel unavailable.

THE RAVEN SPEAKS

U.S. Fantasy 9416

U.K. Fantasy FT509

8/28-30/72

Fat Mama, Alone Again (Naturally), Sandia Chicano (Watermelon Man), It's Too Late, The Raven Speaks, Summer of '42, Reunion at Newport 1972, Bill's Blues.

Al Porcino, Bill Byrne (tp), Charles Davis, John Thomas, Bill Stapleton (tp, flh), Bobby Burgess, Rick Stepton, Harold Garrett (tb), Woody Herman (ss, cl, as), Frank Tiberi, Greg Herbert (ts, ww), Steve Lederer (ts), Tom Anastas (bs), Harold Danko (p), Pat Martino (g), Al Johnson (eb), Joe LaBarbera (d), John Pacheco (cga).

WOODY HERMAN: THUNDERING HERD

U.S. Fantasy F9472

U.K. Fantasy FT 521

1/2-4/74

Lazy Bird, Blues for Poland, What Are You Doing the Rest of Your Life?, Naima, Corazon, Come Saturday Morning, Bass Folk Song.

Bill Byrne (tp), Dave Strahl, Buddy Powers, Bill Stapleton, Tony Klatka (tp, flh), Jim Pugh, Steve Kohlbacher, Harold Garrett (tb), Woody Herman (as, ss), Frank Tiberi, Greg Herbert, Gary Anderson (ts, ww), Jan Konopasek (bs), Andy Laverne (p), Chip Jackson (eb), Ron Davis (d), John Rae (pc).

HERD AT MONTREUX

Fantasy F 9470

7/6/74

I Can't Get Next to You, Superstar, Fanfare for The Common Man, Montevideo, Tantum Ergo, Crosswind.

Exact personnel unavailable.

KING COBRA

Fantasy F 9499
1/7-9/75

King Cobra, Don't You Worry 'Bout a Thing, Spain, Jazzman, Lake Taco, Come Rain or Come Shine, Toothless Grin.
Exact personnel unavailable.

FEELIN' SO BLUE

Fantasy F 9609
1973-75

Echano, Killing Me Softly, Sombrero Sam, Don't Let Me Be Lonely Tonight, Feelin' So Blue, Evergreen, This Time, Brotherhood of Man.
Exact personnel unavailable.

ROAD FATHER

Century CRDD 1080
1/3-4/78

Fire Dance, Duke Ellington's Sound of Love, Woodchopper's Ball, Sunrise Lady, Pavanne, I've Got News for You, Sugar Loaf Mountain, Isn't She Lovely.
Exact personnel unavailable.

TOGETHER: WOODY AND FLIP

Century CR 1090
1/78

Easy Living, How Deep Is the Ocean, I Won't Last a Day Without You, We'll Be Together Again, The Very Thought of You, You Will Be My Music, There Is No Greater Love, The Nearness of You.
Woody Herman (cl, as), Flip Phillips (ts), other personnel unavailable.

CHICK, DONALD, WALTER, WOODROW

Century CR 1110
1/78

Suite for a Hot Band, Green Earrings, Kid Charlemagne, I've Got the News, Aja, FM.
Chick Corea (p), Woody Herman (as, cl), other personnel unavailable.

WOODY AND FRIENDS

Concord CJ 170
9/15/79

Caravan, I Got It Bad, Count Down, Better Get It in Your Soul, Woody'n You, What Are You Doing the Rest of Your Life, Manteca.
Joe Rodriguez, Tim Burke, Kitt Reid (tp), Bill Byrne, Jim Powell (tp, flh), Birch Johnson, Nelson Hinds, Larry Shunk (tb), Woody Herman (ss, as), Frank

Tiberi, Dick Mitchell (ts, ww), Bob Belden (ts), Gary Smulyan (bs), Dave Lalama (p), Dave Larocca (b), Ed Soph (d).

On *What Are You Doing...:* Stan Getz (ts) added as featured soloist.

On *Woody'n You, Manteca:* Dizzy Gillespie, Woody Shaw (tp) and Slide Hampton (tb) added as featured soloists.

CD SELECTIONS

WOODY HERMAN GOLDEN FAVORITES

MCA MCAD 31277
1939-40

Woodchopper's Ball, The Golden Wedding, Who Dat Up Dere, Yardbird Shuffle, Down Under, Indian Boogie Woogie, Blue Flame, Four or Five Times, Irresistable You, Chip's Boogie Woogie, Las Chiapanecas, Woodsheddin' With Woody.

On *Indian Boogie Woogie:* Clarence Willard, Jerry Neary (tp), Joe Bishop (flh), Neil Reid (tb), Woody Herman (cl, as, v), Joe Estren, Ray Hopfner (as), Saxie Mansfield, Pete Johns (ts), Tommy Linchan (p), Hy White (g), Walter Yoder (b), Frank Carlson (d).

On *Woodchopper's Ball:* Mac MacQuordale and Steady Nelson (tp) replace Jerry Neary.

On *Chip's Boogie Woogie, Yardbird Shuffle:* Woody Herman and His Four Chips, Herman (cl, v), Linchan (p), White (g), Yoder (b), Carlson (d).

On *Golden Wedding:* Bob Price, Steady Nelson, Cappy Lewis (tp), Bud Smith, Jesse Ralph, Neil Reid (tb), Woody Herman (cl, as), Herb Tomkins, Bill Vitale (as), Mickey Folus, Saxie Mansfield (ts), Tommy Linchan (p), Hy White (g), Walter Yoder (b), Frank Carlson (d).

On *Blue Flame:* Johnny Owens (tp), Vic Hamann (tb), Eddie Scalzi (as) replace Bob Price, Jesse Ralph and Bill Vitale.

On *Woodsheddin' With Woody:* Carolyn Grey (v).

On *Las Chiapanecas:* Billie Rogers (tp).

On *Four of Five Times, Down Under:* Chuck Peterson, George Seaberg, Cappy Lewis, Billie Rogers (tp), Wally Nims, Tommy Farr, Neil Reid (tb), Woody Herman (cl, as, v), Sam Rubinwitch, Ed Costanza (as), Mickey Folus, Pete Mondello (ts), Lommy Linehan (p), Hy White (g), Walter Yoder (b), Frank Carlson (d).

On *Who Dat Up Dere:* Ray Wetzel, Bobby Guyer, Benny Stabler, Nick Travis, Cappy Lewis (tp), Al Mastren, Ed Kiefer, Eddie Bert (tb), Woody Herman (cl, as, v), Johnny Bothwell, Chuck DiMaggio (as), Pete Mondello, Ben Webster (ts), Skippy DeSair (bs), Dick Kane (p), Hy White (g), Chubby Jackson (b), Cliff Leeman (d).

On *Irresistable You:* Ray Wetzel, Bobby Guyer, Mario Serritello, Neal Hefti (tp), Ed Kiefer, Ed Bennett, Al Esposito (tb), Woody Herman (cl, as, v), Ernie Caceres, Chuck DiMaggio (as), Pete Mondello, Budd Johnson (ts), Skippy DeSair (bs), Ralph Burns (p), Hy White (g), Marjorie Hyams (vb), Chubby Jackson (b), Cliff Leeman (d), Frances Wayne (v).

CRAZY RHYTHM

Garland GRZ 007

The Good Earth, Woodchopper's Ball, It's Coolin' Time, Fire Island, Bamba Samba, Prelude a la Cha Cha, Wild Root, Blue Station, Pillar to Post, Carioca, I Cover the Waterfront, Sinbad the Sailor, Crazy Rhythm.

Exact personnel unavailable.

GIANT STEPS

Fantasy FCD609-9432

4/9-12/73

La Fiesta, A Song for You, Freedom Jazz Dance, The Meaning of the Blues, The First Thing I Do, Think on Me, Giant Steps, A Child Is Born, Bebop and Roses.

Bill Byrne, Larry Pyatt, Gil Rathel, Walt Blanton (tp), Bill Stapleton (tp, flh), Jim Pugh, Geoff Sharp, Harold Garrett (tb), Woody Herman (ss, as, cl), Frank Tiberi, Steve Lederer (ts), Greg Herbert (ts, ww), Harry Kleintank (ts, bs), Andy Laverne (ep), Joe Beck (g), Wayne Darling (b, eb), Ed Soph (d), Ray Barretto (cga).

125TH STREET

Dunhill DZS 005

1945-47

Sweet Lorraine, Blues on Parade, Ain't Misbehavin', Somebody Loves Me, Muskrat Ramble, Exactly Like You, G.I. Jive, Apple Honey, Someday Sweetheart, 1-2-3-4 Jump.

Exact personnel unavailable.

WOODY HERMAN: THE THUNDERING HERDS 1945-1947

CBS CKJ44108

1945-47

(Selections on three original LPs)

VOL. I:

Laura, Apple Honey, I Wonder, Caldonia, Happiness Is Just a Thing Called Joe, Goosey Gander, Northwest Passage, A Kiss Goodnight, I've Got the World on a String, The Good Earth, Put That Ring on My Finger, Bijou, Gee But It's Good to Hold You, Your Father's Moustache, Wild Root, Blowin' Up a Storm.

VOL. II:

Let It Snow, Welcome to My Dream, Panacea, Igor, Steps, Fan It, Nero's Conception, Lost Weekend, Pam, The Sidewalks of Cuba, Lady McGowan's Dream (parts 1 and 2), Romance in the Dark, I Surrender Dear, Someday Sweetheart, At the Woodchopper's Ball.

VOL. III:

Summer Sequence (parts 1 to 3), Everywhere, With Someone New, Wrap Your Troubles in Dreams, Back Talk, Non-Alcoholic, I Told Ya I Love Ya Now Get Out, I've Got News for You, Keen and Peachy, P.S. I Love You.

(Selections on single-LP reissue in 1988 on Columbia Jazz Masterpieces - CJ 44108)

Woodchopper's Ball, Apple Honey, Goosey Gander, Northwest Passage, The Good Earth, A Jug of Wine, Your Father's Moustache, Bijou, Wild Root, Panacea, Back Talk, Non-Alcoholic, The Blues Are Brewing, The Goof and I, Four Brothers, Blue Flame.

On *Laura, Apple Honey, I Wonder, Caldonia, Happiness Is Just a Thing Called Joe, Goosey Gander, Northwest Passage, A Kiss Goodnight, I've Got the World on a String:* Ray Wetzel, Carl Warwick, Chuck Frankhauser, Pete Candoli, Sonny Berman (tp), Ed Kiefer, Ralph Pfeffner, Bill Harris (tp), Woody Herman (cl, as, v) Sam Marowitz, John La Porta (as), Pete Mondello, Flip Phillips (ts), Skippy DeSair (bs), Marjorie Hyams (vb), Ralph Burns (p), Billy Bauer (g), Chubby Jackson (b), Dave Tough (d), Frances Wayne (v).

On *The Good Earth, Put That Ring on My Finger, Bijou, Gee But It's Good to Hold You, Your Father's Moustache, Wild Root:* Ray Linn, Neal Hefti, Conte Candoli, Pete Candoli, Sonny Berman (tp), Ed Kiefer, Ralph Pfeffner, Bill Harris (tb), Woody Herman (cl, as, v), Sam Marowitz, John La Porta (as), Pete Mondello, Flip Phillips (ts), Skippy DesSair (bs), Tony Aless (p), Billy Bauer (g), Chubby Jackson (b), Dave Tough (d), Frances Wayne (v).

On *Blowin' Up a Storm, Let It Snow, Welcome to My Dream:* Irv Lewis, Neal Hefti, Shorty Rogers, Pete Candoli, Sonny Berman (tp), Ed Kiefer, Ralph Pfeffner, Bill Harris (tb), Woody Herman (cl, as, v), Sam Marowitz, John La Porta (as), Mickey Folus, Flip Phillips (ts), Sam Rubinwitch (bs), Tony Aless (p), Billy Bauer (g), Chubby Jackson (b), Don Lamond (d), Frances Wayne (v).

On *Panacea:* Conrad Gozzo, Irvin Markowitz, Shorty Rogers, Pete Candoli, Sonny Berman (tp), Ed Kiefer, Ralph Pfeffner, Bill Harris (tb), Woody Herman (cl, as, v), Sam Marowitz, John La Porta (as), Mickey Folus, Flip Phillips (ts), Sam Rubinwitch (bs), Red Norvo (vb), Tony Aless (p), Billy Bauer (g), Chubby Jackson (b), Don Lamond (d).

On *Igor, Steps, Fan It, Nero's Conception, Lost Weekend, Pam:* Herman and The Woodchoppers, with Sonny Berman (tp), Bill Harris (tb), Herman (cl, v), Flip Phillips (ts), Red Norvo (vb), Jimmy Rowles (p), Billy Bauer (g), Chubby Jackson (b), Don Lamond (d).

On *The Sidewalks of Cuba, Lady McGowan's Dream, Romance in the*

Dark, Summer Sequence, Everywhere, With Someone New, Wrap Your Troubles..., Back Talk: Conrad Gozzo, Cappy Lewis, Shorty Rogers, Pete Candoli, Sonny Berman (tp), Ed Kiefer, Ralph Pfeffner, Neil Reid, Bill Harris (tb), Woody Herman (cl, as), Sam Marowitz, John La Porta (as), Mickey Folus, Flip Phillips (ts), Sam Rubinwitch (bs), Red Norvo (vb), Jimmy Rowles (p), Chuck Wayne (g), Joe Mondragon (b), Don Lamond (d), Mary Ann McCall (v).

On *I Surrender Dear, Someday Sweetheart:* Herman and The Woodchoppers, with Sonny Berman (tp), Bill Harris (tb), Herman (cl), Flip Phillips (ts), Red Norvo (vb), Jimmy Rowles (p), Chuck Wayne (g), Joe Mondragon (b), Don Lamond (d).

On *Woodchopper's Ball, Non-Alcoholic:* Conrad Gozzo, Chuck Peterson, Cappy Lewis, Al Porcino, Bob Peck (tp), Ed Kiefer, Ralph Pfeffner, Bill Harris (tb), Woody Herman (cl), Sam Marowitz, John La Porta (as), Flip Phillips (ts), Sam Rubinwitch (bs), Jimmy Rowles (p), Chuck Wayne (g), Joe Mondragon (b), Don Lamond (d).

On *I Told Ya I Love Ya..., I've Got News for You, Keen and Peachy, The Goof and I, Lazy Lullaby, Four Brothers, Summer Sequence, P.S. I Love You:* Bernie Glow, Stan Fis-helson, Irvin Markowitz, Shorty Rogers, Ernie Royal (tp), Ollie Wilson, Earl Swope, Bob Swift (tb), Woody Herman (cl, as, v), Sam Marowitz (as), Herbie Steward (ts, as), Stan Getz, Zoot Sims (ts), Serge Chaloff (bs), Fred Otis (p), Gene Sargent (g), Walter Yoder (b), Don Lamond (d), Mary Ann McCall (v).

WOODY HERMAN: COMPACT JAZZ

Verve 835 319-2
1962-63

The Good Earth, Don't Get Around Much Anymore, Bijou, Body and Soul, Leo the Lion, Makin' Whoopee, Camel Walk, Apple Honey, Pee Wee Blues, The Preacher, Sidewalks of Cuba, Golden Wedding, Caldonia, Blue Flame.
Exact personnel unavailable.

WOODY HERMAN LIVE IN ANTIBES 1965

Fr. Concert FCD 117
1965

Blue Flame, The Preacher, Wailing in the Wood, Hallelujah Time, Satin Doll, Somewhere, Four Brothers, Early Autumn, Medley: Rose Room/In a Mellow Tone, Don't Get Around Much Anymore, 23 Red, Northwest Passage, Watermelon Man, I Remember Clifford, Caldonia.
Exact personnel unavailable.

WOODY HERMAN 40TH ANNIVERSARY AT CARNEGIE HALL

RCA Bluebird 6878-2RB
11/26/76

Blue Flame (Herman acknowledgement), Apple Honey [feat. Flip Phillips (ts), Jim Pugh, Phil Wilson (tb), Pete Candoli (tp)], Sweet and Lovely [feat. Phillips], Four Brothers [feat. Jimmy Giuffre (bs), Stan Getz, Al Cohn, Zoot Sims (ts)], Brotherhood of Man [feat. Pete Candoli, Conte Candoli (tp)], Early Autumn [feat. Herman (as), Ralph Burns (p), Stan Getz (ts)], Wrap Your Troubles in Dreams [feat. Mary Ann McCall (v), Phillips (ts), Herman (cl)], Everywhere [feat. Pugh (tb)], Bijou [feat. Wilson (tb)], Cousins [feat. Cohn, Giuffre, Getz (ts), Jimmy Rowles (p)], Blue Serge [feat. Getz (ts)], Blue Getz Blues [feat. Getz (ts)], Caldonia [Herman (v)].

Collective personnel: Pete Candoli, Conte Candoli, Alan Vizutti, Nelson Hatt, John Hoffman, Dennis Dotson, Bill Byrne, Danny Styles (tp), Phil Wilson, Jim Pugh, Dale Kirkland, Jim Daniels (tb), Sam Marowitz (as) Stan Getz, Flip Phillips, Zoot Sims, Jimmy Giuffre, Frank Tiberi, Gary Anderson, Joe Lovano, Al Cohn (ts), John Oslawski (bs), Woody Herman (cl, as, v), Jimmy Rowles, Nat Pierce, Ralph Burns, Pat Coil (p), Billy Bauer (g), Chubby Jackson, Rusy Holloway (b), Don Lamond, Jake Hanna, Dan D'Imperio (d).

On *Wrap Your Troubles in Dreams:* Mary Ann McCall (v).

LIVE AT THE CONCORD JAZZ FESTIVAL

Concord
CCD-4191
8/81

Things Ain't What They Used to Be, Theme In Search of a Movie, Midnight Run, You Are So Beautiful, John Brown's Other Body, Especially for You, North Beach Breakdown, The Dolphin, Lemon Drop.

Bill Stapleton, Brian O'Flaherty, George Rabbai, Scott Wagstaff, Mark Lewis (tp), Gene Smith, Larry Shunk, John Fedchock (tb), Woody Herman (cl, as), Paul McGinley, Bill Ross, Randy Russell (ts, ww), Mike Brignola (bs), John Oddo (p, ep), Mike Hall (b, eb), Dave Ratajczak (d, pc).

On *Things Ain't What They Used to Be:* Al Cohn (ts) added.
On *The Dolphin:* Stan Getz (ts) added as featured soloist.
On *Lemon Drop:* Scat bop vocal by George Rabbai.

THE WOODY HERMAN BIG BAND - WORLD CLASS

Concord CCD-4240
9/82

Four Brothers, The Claw, Peanut Vendor, Crystal Silence, Greasy Sack Blues, Perdido, Rockin' Chair, Woody's Lament.

On *Four Brothers, The Claw:* Al Cohn, Med Flory, Sal Nistico and Flip Phillips (ts) added.
On *Peanut Vendor, Crystical Silence:* Jeff Hamilton (pc) added.
On *Perdido:* Phillips (ts) added.
On *Rockin' Chair:* Herman and George Rabbai (v).
On *Woody's Lament:* Cohn and Nistico (ts) added.

50TH ANNIVERSARY TOUR

Concord CCD-4302

3/86

It Don't Mean a Thing (If It Ain't Got That Swing), What's New, Pools, Blues for Red, Conga, Central Park West, Fried Buzzard, Epistrophy.

Roger Ingram, Les Lovitt, Mark Lewis, Ron Stout, Bill Byrne (tp, flh), John Fedchock, Paul McKee, Mark Lusk (tb), Woody Herman (cl, ss), Frank Tiberi, Dave Riekenberg, Jerry Pinter (ts), Mike Brignola (bs), Brad Williams (p), Lynn Seaton (b), Jim Rupp (d).

WOODY'S GOLD STAR

Concord CCD-4330

3/87

Battle Royal, Woody's Gold Star, Mambo Rockland, 'Round Midnight, The Great Escape, Dig, Rose Room/In a Mellow Tone, Watermelon Man, Samba Song.

Roger Ingram, George Baker, Jim Powell, Ron Stout, Bill Byrne (tp), John Fedchock, Paul McKee, Joe Barati (tb), Woody Herman (cl, ss), Frank Tiberi, Dave Riekenberg, Jerry Pinter (ts), Mike Brignola (bs), Joel Weiskopf (p), Dave Carpenter (b, eb), Dave Miller (d), Pete Escovedo (pc), Poncho Sanchez (cga), Ramon Banda (timbales).

EBONY: WOODY HERMAN ORCH. - RICHARD STOLTZMAN

RCA 6486-2-RL

5/11-12/87

American Medley: Amazing Grace, America the Beautiful, Battle Hymn of the Republic; Come Sunday, Apple Honey, Ebony Concerto, Igor, Stories From the West Side: Somewhere, Cool, Maria, Something's Coming; Waltz for Woody, Cousins.

Roger Ingram, Diane White, Greg Gisbert, Ron Stout, Bill Byrne (tp), John Fedchock, Paul McKee, Joe Barati (tb), Richard Stoltzman (cl) Frank Tiberi, Dave Riekenberg, Jerry Pinter, Mike Brignola (ww), Joel Weiskopf (p), Dave Carpenter (b), Dave Miller (d), Alex Brofsky (Fr. horn), Sarah Voinow (harp), Howard Alden (g).

INDEX

LaVergne, TN USA
17 March 2011
220586LV00007B/87/P